D0742264

# LEARNERS
## AND
# DISCERNERS

# LEARNERS
# AND
# DISCERNERS

## *A Newer Criticism*

Discussions of
Modern Literature by

HARRY LEVIN
JOHN FREDERICK NIMS
R. W. B. LEWIS
HUGH KENNER
IHAB HASSAN

Selected and Edited by ROBERT SCHOLES

THE UNIVERSITY PRESS OF VIRGINIA
CHARLOTTESVILLE

"The Dismemberment of Orpheus" was first published
in the *American Scholar* (Summer 1963) and the copyright was assigned to Ihab Hassan in 1963.

"Art in a Closed Field" first appeared in the *Virginia
Quarterly Review* (Autumn 1962) and was copyrighted
in 1962.

"Symbolism and Fiction" was published in 1956 by the
University of Virginia.

*First published 1964*

Library of Congress Catalog Card Number: 64-13303

Printed in the United States of America by
THE WILLIAM BYRD PRESS, INC.

# PREFACE

ALL five of the essays in this collection were delivered as lectures at the University of Virginia in the series established in 1946 by Urban Joseph Peters Rushton and continued in his honor after his death in 1949. Born in Birmingham, Alabama, in 1915, educated at Princeton, Harvard, and Cambridge universities, Peters Rushton served the University of Virginia as a member of the English Department and as Assistant Dean of the College of Arts and Sciences. These, his public services, were augmented by generous gifts to the University library—given always with the stipulation that his name not be made public. The lecture series which he founded at his own expense has been continued through the generosity of his family. The Peters Rushton Seminars have brought many of the most vigorous and distinguished of modern critics to Virginia. In this volume are published some of the most provocative and significant lectures delivered in the past few years.

This collection has been subtitled "A Newer Criticism" not in order to make a bad joke at the expense of the "new critics," who have made a valuable contribution to the study of literature, but to draw attention to the fact that these writers, diverse as their critical views are, stand on a common ground that is different from the ground occupied by their predecessors. Most obviously, the new-critical tendency to isolate literature from its biographical and historical context is here reversed. Every critic in this volume brings some special knowledge to bear on the material under discussion, drawing on biographical data, literary history, or such extra-literary fields as mathematics and philosophy. And of all these sources literary history is the most important. We find that in order to discuss Salinger we must consider Ovid; in order to discuss Beckett we must consider Flaubert; to discuss Yeats we must consider Castiglione. We find that Hart Crane must be seen against a spectrum of clowns from Percival to Charlie Chaplin, and that the way to Hemingway's "Big Two-hearted River" is via the Liffey and the Nile.

The critics in this volume are all trying to consider literary works as things-in-themselves, but as things which are dependent on and related to a literary and cultural tradition. The essays are all on modern literature, but the literature is always seen in relation to contemporary culture and our cultural heritage. In the first essay, Professor Levin reminds us that the critic of fiction ought to bring to his task the discipline and learning of the iconographer; that no critic can talk about "symbols" intelligently unless he understands that they are elements of cultural significance as well as devices of art. He calls for a newer criticism which will combine the learning of historical scholarship with the discernment of the "new criticism." The essays which follow are all attempts, in one way or another, to provide this combination, and in doing so to justify criticism as an intellectual discipline. They are, in a sense, not only essays in criticism but essays on criticism as well. They are, to some extent, about the function of criticism at the present time in its continuing dialogue with the literature of the present time. These critics stand in relation to the difficult and exciting literature of our own day not as judges but as advocates; their aim is not explication, merely, but understanding—which is a deeper, richer, more complex, and more worthwhile endeavor.

ROBERT SCHOLES

*Charlottesville, Virginia*
*July 1963*

# CONTENTS

# SYMBOLISM AND FICTION

by

HARRY LEVIN

A FEW YEARS AGO we welcomed to our Department at Harvard a colleague who had never before taught English literature. As a poet he had practised it, as a lawyer he had once taught law, and as Assistant Secretary of State he may even have prepared himself to cope with the complexities of academic life. Why should I not mention the honored name of Archibald MacLeish? Mr. MacLeish was anxious to meet the minds of the college generation, and incidentally to test the observation that William Faulkner had supplanted Ernest Hemingway as their literary idol. His first assignment required his class, as a sort of touchstone, to read and report on Mr. Hemingway's "Big Two-Hearted River." They had not read it, but you have, and you remember that it is hardly a story at all; it is simply a sketch about a boy who goes fishing. Its striking quality is the purity of its feeling, its tangible grasp of sensuous immediacy, the physical sensation that Mr. Hemingway is so effective at putting into prose. The students did not seem to feel this quality. They liked the story, they wrote about it at length, but, in their protocols, to a man, they allegorized it. Each of those fish that Nick Adams had jerked out of Big Two-Hearted River bore for them a mystical significance, which varied according to its interpreter— Freudian or Jungian, Kierkegaardian or Kafkaesque. May I leave these silvery, slippery trout dangling there in the water to incarnate the fascination and the elusiveness of our subject?

American literature would all be childishness, the innocent wonderment of the schoolroom—according to one of its most perceptive interpreters, D. H. Lawrence—if it did not invite us to look beneath its bland surface and to find a diabolic inner meaning. The reaction of Professor MacLeish's students might suggest that we do not enjoy the surfaces enough, that we have become too morbidly preoccupied with the subliminal. In our restless search for universals, we may be losing sight of particulars: of the so-called quiddity, that "whatness" which characterizes a work of art, the truth of an object to its peculiar self. Literature is not a game of charades. Yet Lawrence's reinterpretation helped to rescue, out of the indiscriminate attic of children's books, the greatest classic in American literature; and *Moby Dick* has plenty of deviltry at its core. When a lightning-rod man intruded upon Mark Twain, the upshot was a humoristic sketch. When a lightning-rod man intruded upon Herman Melville, the consequence became part of his lifelong quarrel with organized religion. It may now remain for some intrepid young allegorist to demonstrate in some little magazine that Mark Twain's sketch is nothing less than a cryptographic adumbration of a Rosicrucian tract.

At this juncture it may prove useful to be reminded that *Moby Dick* itself, like "Big Two-Hearted River," is a simple story about a fishing trip. Basically, it is just another yarn about the big fish that got away. So is Mr. Hemingway's last book, *The Old Man and the Sea*, even though critics have seen themselves symbolized in the sharks that prey on the Old Man's gigantic catch. *Moby Dick*, at all events, is a whopper, and like all whoppers, it has the capacity to be expanded and elaborated *ad infinitum*. In the process of elaboration, Melville has introduced his linked analogies and dark similitudes, sometimes deliberately and, it would also seem, sometimes intuitively. He himself seemed scarcely conscious of certain implications which Nathaniel Hawthorne pointed out, and which thereupon fell into place, as Melville acknowledged, in "the part-and-parcel allegoricalness of the whole." (Or did he write "of the whale"? Melville's handwriting, in his famous letter to Mrs. Hawthorne, is indeterminate at this crucial point.) One of his chapters, anatomizing the beached skeleton of a whale, tells us that some of its smaller vertebrae have been carried away to make children's rattles. And so, he goes on to moralize, almost anticipating the reception of his book, so the most momentous enterprises can taper off into child's play.

Mr. Faulkner, being our contemporary, has not suffered very much from the innocence of his readers. On the contrary, the title of his novel, *A Fable*, proclaims his own ambition to universalize a message of some sort, impelled perhaps by the sense of international responsibility that seems to go along with the Nobel Prize. But let us revert to a more modest example of his story-telling skill, with which we may feel more at home, *The Bear*. This is another story about a hunting trip. It sticks to his region and it securely belongs, along with *The Adventures of Huckleberry Finn* and *The Red Badge of Courage*, among those wonderful American stories in which a boy reaches manhood through some rite of passage, some baptism of fire, an initiation into experience. We may not have noticed, and we should therefore be grateful for the critical comment that points it out, a possible resemblance between the youthful Ike McCaslin and the epic heroes of Homer and Vergil. But we may be less grateful than puzzled when the same Kenyon Critic informs us that *The Bear* is an allegory of "the transition from pagan to Christian culture, if not from the Old to the New Testament." We may even begin to suspect that the commentator lacks a sense of proportion, if not a sense of humor.

Needless to say, these lacks would not be considered serious enough to disqualify him from practising criticism as it is frequently practised today. Criticism is a child of the time, and it changes as times change. The catchwords of critics have tended to echo the ideals of their respective periods. Thus a whole epoch is summed up in the term "decorum," and another by the shibboleth "sublime." What is our key-word? "Ambiguity" is not my own suggestion, it is an obvious recommendation from our contemporary masters of critical terminology. Their stronghold, be it Axel's castle or Kafka's, is not the old allegorical castle of love or war, of perseverance or indolence; it is a citadel of ambiguity. Since the numerous types of ambiguity presuppose as many levels of meaning, it might be more up-to-date to call this castle a skyscraper, and to call our typologists of ambiguity—borrowing a compendious adjective from *Finnegans Wake*—"hierarchitectitiptitoploftical." As an instance of such hierarchitectitiptitoploftical criticism, without pretending to be citing at random, I might cite a recent interpretation of James Joyce's *A Portrait of the Artist as a Young Man.* Here at the outset Cranly, the friend of the artist, is said to be not only John the Baptist but likewise Judas and Pilate—a wide and exacting and not exactly compatible range of roles for a secondary character.

Part of the difficulty would seem to spring from the critic's addiction to the copula. Some of our literary reviews, in this respect, might just as well be written in Basic English. Suggestive allusions tend to become flat assertions. Something, instead of suggesting some other thing, somehow *is* that other thing; it cannot mean, it must be. Everything must be stated as an equation, without recognizing degrees of relationship or the differences between allusion and fact. Now, as the name of his protagonist indicates, Joyce is fond of alluding to prototypes. Cranly is ironically linked with John the Baptist as a kind of predecessor; and to the extent to which every betrayer of his friend is a Judas and every avoider of moral responsibility is a Pilate, he may be said to have momentarily figured in both of those positions. But what are we then to make of the Artist as a Young Man? There is a sense in which the life of every good Christian is, or should be, an imitation of Christ. But Stephen Dedalus expressly chooses to imitate Satan: *"Non serviam!"* The comment is therefore not an ambiguity nor an ambivalence nor a tension nor an irony nor a paradox. It is a contradiction or, to use a very old-fashioned term, an impertinence, and there are times when reason can do no more than imitate Dr. Johnson and kick the stone.

Such interpretations are dismissed as "cabbalistics" by the introduction to one of the many current studies of Franz Kafka. But when we turn from this introduction to the study itself, having been all but convinced that its author is uniquely sane and that Kafka's other commentators are uniformly mad, we find that he too has a frenzied glint in his eye and a cabbalistic theory of his own: all of Kafka is to be explained by the incidence of the number two. Two is an important number, of course, when we come to think about it, and when we start to look for it, it appears to be so ubiquitous that it explains not only Kafka but everything else. The only matter it does not explain is the difference between Kafka and everything else. And that, I fear, is the trouble with much that passes for psychoanalytic criticism: it reduces our vocabulary of symbols to a few which are so crudely fundamental and so monotonously recurrent that they cannot help the critic to perform his primary function, which is still, I take it, to discriminate. Nature abounds in protuberances and apertures. Convexities and concavities, like Sir Thomas Browne's quincunxes, are everywhere. The forms they compose are not always enhanced or illuminated by reading our sexual obsessions into them.

Isolating text from context in the name of "close reading," we can easily be led astray. So sensible a critic as Edmund Wilson has argued that Henry James's "Turn of the Screw" should be read as a psychological projection of its governess's frustrations. Subsequently it has been shown by Professor Robert L. Wolff, a professional historian on a Jamesian holiday, that the manifest content of the alleged fantasy came from a sentimental illustration in a Christmas annual to which James had also contributed. What is needed today perhaps, what readers and writers might well join together in forming, would be a Society for the Protection of Symbols from Critics. But I do not want to labor a point which is, indeed, that all too many points may have been labored already. Having labored a little in the symbolistic vineyard, I share the curiosities and admire the ingenuities of many of my fellow laborers. If these remarks have the intonations of a *caveat*, they should also have the overtones of a *mea culpa*. When, however, this hieratic tendency draws back upon itself the leveling criticism of the philistines who are always with us, thereby exacerbating the war of attrition between the quarterlies and the weeklies, we must all be concerned one way or another.

A primrose by a river's brim is, obviously, one thing to J. Donald Adams and quite another thing to Kenneth Burke. For the leveling critic, the flower in the crannied wall may be simply that and nothing more. A rose itself, the emblem of romance and so much more, the *rosa sempiterna* of Dante, the *rosa mystica* of Hopkins or Yeats, the garden of T. S. Eliot's agony, the thorn of which Rilke may actually have died in aromatic pain—well, a rose is a rose is a rose. And *Moby Dick* is a book which exists on a plane of comparison with the novels of Captain Marryat. Without capitulating to that simplistic view, we could well afford to concede that not every literary surface happens to mask a darker meaning. Every work of art may be a form of symbolic action, as Mr. Burke keeps patiently reminding us (and behind the reminder stands Coleridge's conception of the artist as a creator of symbols). When Hamlet could not accuse Claudius directly, he approached him by means of the play within the play—"tropically." So Ernst Jünger, during the Nazi regime, was able to attack it symbolically in his fantastic tale, *From the Marble Cliffs*. But there are symbols and symbols. "My tropes are not tropes," says King Media to the poet Babbalanja in Melville's *Mardi*, "but yours are." That is the issue: when is a trope not a trope, and what is it then?

It should do us no harm to admit that art continues to have its simpler vehicles, such as love lyrics or works of sculpture, designed to convey feelings rather than ideas. When Mr. MacLeish's students dredged up such grimly subaqueous intimations from the limpid waters of the Big Two-Hearted River, they were essentially engaged in revealing themselves. Furthermore, they were reflecting the outlook of our age—which, as it looks back toward the nineteen-twenties from the vantagepoint of a full generation afterward —seems to be looking across an enormous gulf. Writing at the end of that fabulous decade, Mr. Wilson terminated his *Axel's Castle* with a kind of farewell to the symbolists: to Yeats and Joyce and Proust and several other supreme individualists, and to those rare artificial worlds of their private creation. But symbolism proved much too deeply rooted to take the hint and retire. In the meanwhile, a call for a "science of symbolism" had been issued by C. K. Ogden and I. A. Richards. Exploring the personal and the collective unconscious, Freud and Jung had shown how primitive myths survive through oneiric fantasies. Furthermore, public events have intervened in our lives to strengthen the authority of symbols. Hence the movement, broadening its base, has been going forward—or is it backward? For symbolism, in the Hegelian world view, characterizes the earliest phase of culture.

One of the signs of revival has been the popularity of Suzanne Langer's *Philosophy in a New Key*, with its stimulating argument that modern logic, semantics, metaphysics, and various schools of thought in the social sciences run parallel to the course of symbolism among the arts. But the key in which all this is pitched,

by virtue of Mrs. Langer's synesthetic metaphor, is
by no means new. It is so old that we might properly
call it a "mode," and it leads us back to other modes
of thinking which are rather prelogical than logical,
rather magical than scientific, rather transcendental
than empirical. Mrs. Langer's two philosophical masters, Ernst Cassirer and Alfred North Whitehead,
were both profoundly aware that symbolism is inherent in the very processes of language and thought.
So was Quintilian: *"Paene quicquid loquimur figura
est."* We could hardly speak or think or vote without
symbols; we live and die by them; we should hesitate
to cross the street at a traffic intersection, were it not
for their unambiguous accord. All art, in this sense,
is more or less symbolic. More or less, and whether
it is more symbolic or less may be determined by historical as well as by esthetic considerations.

Take an illustration which William Butler Yeats
admired because it happened to be "out of nature,"
because it belonged to "the artifice of eternity." Take
"such a form as Grecian goldsmiths make"—a Byzan-
tine icon. Such a religious image had to be stylized
and conventionalized along the lines that were sanctioned and prescribed by the Church of the East. Its
style could be considered more symbolic than the
painting of the West; for western painters, freed from
the conventions and prescriptions and restrictions of
Iconoclastic dogma, could come closer and closer to
life, even as material actuality was becoming secular
and realistic. At the eastern extreme, the taboo of the
Jewish and Mohammedan religions against the making of graven images sponsored an art which was

decorative and functional but not precisely significant, as in a prayer-rug. "In a symbol," wrote Thomas Carlyle in his handbook for symbolists, *Sartor Resartus*, "there is both concealment and revelation." But if everything were revealed, then nothing would be symbolized; and if everything were concealed, then too nothing would be symbolized. Thus a symbol is a sort of excluded middle between what we know and what we do not know—or better, as Carlyle put it, a meeting point between the finite and the infinite.

Art is always an imitation, never quite the real thing. It cannot represent without symbolizing. By its devices of synecdoche or metonymy, it gives us the part for the whole or the attribute for the object. It never gives us a perfect replica; on the other hand, it never gives us a complete abstraction. What has been ineptly termed "non-objective painting" proves if nothing else that there is really no such thing as pure design. In the dramatic moralities Vanity is a highly feminine creature and the Vice is full of boyish mischief. Life itself is bound to be mixed up with any artistic representation of it; yet even the "slice of life" of the naturalists had to be framed by symbolic conceptions, as in the fiction of Emile Zola or his American disciple, Frank Norris. Think of Norris's titles, *The Pit*, *The Octopus*, not to mention the monstrous tooth of McTeague. Banish the symbol, and it returns as a simile: the mine shaft transformed by *Germinal* into a perpetually crouching beast. The London fog, with its natural aura of obfuscation, becomes a metaphorical vehicle for Dickens's critique of the law courts in *Bleak House*. And Flaubert concentrates with such intensity on the details of materialistic circumstance that, in *A Simple Heart*, the stuffed parrot of his old servant woman is apotheosized into the Paraclete.

Generally speaking, art seems to oscillate between two poles, the symbolistic and the realistic, or, we might say, the typical and the individual. In its westward movement it has kept pace with the development of human individuality. In its eastward purview it glances backward toward Byzantium, and toward an order of mind which derives its strength from the opposing principle of typicality. This polarity is recognized by philosophy in the habitual problem of the One and the Many, and it has innumerable repercussions in the political and socio-cultural areas. Through some such oscillation we have been moving, at least until lately, in the direction set by the Greeks. A humanistic literature such as theirs is not primarily regulated by symbolism. Homer and Sophocles made use of symbols, yes; but the *Odyssey* is a story about a man named "Odysseus"; it is not an ironic commentary upon a day in the life of a man named "Leopold Bloom." Oedipus, since he verily married his mother, was presumably the one recorded man who did not suffer from the frustrations of the Oedipus complex. The world of Odysseus and Oedipus was concrete; it was here and now as long as it lasted. Ages with less pride in the dignity of mankind would preach contempt for this world, along with hope for another and better one hereafter. The visible things of this earth, in the doctrine of Saint Paul, shadow forth the invisible things of God. As Christopher Cranch, the

transcendentalist poet, expressed it: "Nature is but
a scroll; God's handwriting thereon." It is held that
the artist, like the prophet, should have the insight to
read and translate these divine hieroglyphics. Such is
the state of mind that makes for symbolism, both in
creating and in interpreting a hermetic art.

The two points of view, the otherwordly and the
humanistic, clashed in the conflict between Christian
asceticism and the pagan classics which Saint Augustine resolved by formulating a masterly distinction between the spirit and the letter. If the letter kills, the
spirit brings new life, and if a text is literally profane,
it may be read figuratively and endowed retrospectively with a spiritual significance. *The Song of Songs*
reads suspiciously like an erotic poem, yet the Rabbis
admitted it to the sacred canon by pronouncing it to
be an allegory of God's love for Israel. Similarly the
Fathers, for whom the Old Testament prefigured the
New, accepted it as an expression of Christ's love for
the Church. Following Augustine, through this retro-
active procedure known as "figuration," the *Aeneid*
could be taken as a pilgrimage of the soul adventuring
among divers moral hazards. Thereafter Dante could
take Vergil as his guide for a series of literal adventures through the next world. Dante, as he acknowledged, was also following Saint Thomas Aquinas,
who—in answering the preliminary questions of his
*Summa Theologica*—had sustained the doctrine that
although the Scriptures were literally true, they could
be interpreted as figures on three ascending levels of
spiritual meaning.

But though the *Divine Comedy* is polysemous, as

it is expounded in Dante's dedicatory letter to Can Grande della Scala, the poem cannot pretend to literal truth; the Florentine poet, after all, was making believe that he himself had journeyed through Hell and Purgatory and Paradise; the "allegory of poets" is not the "allegory of theologians." The next step would be taken by the more worldly Boccaccio, who in his life of Dante supported the validity of poetic truth. Elsewhere he went even farther, with the affirmation that theology is God's poetry. It has remained for latter-day symbolists to round out the cycle by affirming that poetry is man's theology. With the humanism of the Renaissance and the Enlightenment, the other world seems gradually to recede. Nominalistic reality shifts to the foreground; things are valued for themselves, and not for what they may prefigure. The shift from the type to the individual has its protagonist in *Doctor Faustus*, Marlowe's early sketch for Goethe's portrayal of modernism in action. Faustus is one poet who is not content to compare his mistress with famous beauties. Metaphors will not do and symbols are not enough; he must attain the object of his comparison. He must have the one and only Helen of Troy, and he does so *in propria persona*, but the reality proves to be as elusive as the symbol.

Poetry with its metaphors, metaphysics with its analogies, bridge a gap between seen and unseen worlds. The breakdown of the bridge is that dissociation of which Mr. Eliot has written so feelingly; and it is more than a "dissociation of sensibility," it is a break in the whole chain of being. Hume's critique of analogy might be regarded, under this aspect, as a philosophical counterpart of neoclassical poetic diction. A symbol, on the other hand, is a connecting link between two different spheres, for the original word in Greek meant throwing together, a violent fusion, the very act of association. When man stands upon his own feet, proudly conscious of the achievements of his fellow men, he lives most fully and his art embodies the fullness of his life, his basic sense of reality. Then the *Aeneid* is not a *pélérinage de la vie humaine* but the epic of a hero; the *Song of Songs* is not an allegory but a chant of love; and Shakespeare's tragedies are dramas of physical action and psychological conflict, not ballets of bloodless images or ceremonials for a dying god. In times which seem to be out of joint, when man is alienated from his environment, the heroic seems less immediately attainable and love itself may dim to a Platonic vision. A failure of nerve is accompanied by a retreat from reality.

Arthur Symons characterized the symbolistic movement of the nineteenth century as a perfervid effort to escape from materialism. It is much easier to comprehend what the symbolists were escaping from than what they were escaping to. Their problem was, and it certainly remains, to establish a viable set of intimate associations with another sphere. Some of them felt they had solved it personally through religious conversion; others frankly used their visionary imaginations, often abetted by stimulants and even by mental disorders. Whereas the traditional symbolist had abstracted objects into ideas, the self-proclaimed *Symboliste*—as Jean Moréas announced in his manifesto of 1886—sought to invest the idea in concrete form. Hence his emphasis was on the object itself rather than its conceivable signification, on the denseness of the imagery rather than the pattern of the thought, on concealment rather than revelation, in Carlyle's terms. But since the symbol was never clearly acknowledged as the key to any higher plane of existence, poets could not be blamed when it became a fetish cultivated for its own sake. Literature could not be expected to transcend itself by its own bootstraps, and yet, with Mallarmé the esthetic process became the principal subject for symbolization. So it is with Proust; but when it is manifested in connoisseurship of ecclesiastical architecture, the symbols are already fraught with a transcendence of their own.

The unvoiced premise of *Symbolisme*, which is not far from that of orthodox mysticism, had been handed on by the German idealists to the New England transcendentalists. For Baudelaire, moving out of the woods of naturalism back toward the church, nature was a temple with trees for pillars. Man walks through this forest of symbols which seem to know him better than he knows them, and the words he hears there are confused. *"Les parfums, les couleurs, et les sons se répondent."* Color and sound and other sensory impressions are linked together through correspondences, associative patterns whose final sanction is not discernible to the senses. Some of these were suggested by Rimbaud in his well-known sonnet on the vowels, but not everyone would accept his linkages. Different sounds would suggest different colors to different readers, and that is the essential dilemma of *Symbol-*

*isme*. For all its efforts to reorder the universe, to categorize the diversity of experience, its influence has been unregenerately individualistic. Remy de Gourmont, the critical interpreter of the movement, aptly presents it as, among other things, the ultimate expression of individualism in art.

How far it stands apart from its medieval prototype might be measured by consulting the *Rationale* of Durandus, the thirteenth-century manual of Christian symbolism as embodied in the sacramentalism of the Catholic church. Living tradition was and is practised daily there through the cruciform structure of the edifice, its orientation, ritual, and liturgy, the relation of the church year to the life of Christ, the re-enactment of the last supper in the Eucharist. Through that rite of communion the paschal lamb, originally the sacrifice of the Jewish Passover, had become the commonest symbol for Jesus. The audience at fifteenth-century Wakefield, witnessing their *Second Shepherd's Play*, could not irreverently grasp a serio-comic parallel between the infant in the manger and the stolen sheep of the farcical underplot. This is an authoritative example of the technique of symbolic association. Conversely, we witness the effect of dissociation in *Madame Bovary*, when the great Cathedral of Rouen looks reprovingly down upon the lovers fleeing in their cab, and its disregarded sermons in stones exemplify all the values that Emma and Léon are flouting. It is a far cry from George Herbert's *Temple* to Baudelaire's.

"A symbol remains vital," the late Karl Vossler has written, "only when its representation is accompanied

by faith." The number seven was no abstraction for
Dante; behind it loomed the power of the Seven Sacra-
ments, the Seven Deadly Sins, the Seven Gifts of the
Holy Ghost. But when we turn away from the super-
natural, in naturalistic suspension of belief, what, if
anything, are we to make of Thomas Mann's conjura-
tions with the same digit in *The Magic Mountain*?
The seven chapters of the novel itself, the seven tables
in the dining room of the Berghof sanitorium, which
has seven letters in its name, as have its seven principal guests in their names, and all the recurrent mul-
tiples of seven—these are endowed with no more
efficacy than the novelist's deliberate manipulation of
coincidence. Whereas, if we now reconsider our fish,
we find that it is alphabetically associated with the
initial letters of the Greek words for "Jesus Christ,
Son of God, the Savior," which can be read acrosti-
cally as "*ichthys*." As such it served in the catacombs,
where overt symbols would have been dangerous,
to conceal the Christian revelation. In the terms of
Durandus, it was a positive rather than a natural symbol, or as Yeats would say, arbitrary rather than inherent.

It is the inherent, the natural symbol that Coleridge
seems to have in mind when he asserts that it always
partakes of that reality which it renders intelligible.
The cross or the lamb, as opposed to the fish, may
well be termed an emblem, as distinguished from a
sign. But Saint Augustine can transform a sign into
an emblem when he mystically envisions Jesus Christ
as a fish swimming through the depths of mortality.
This distinction between emblems and signs corre-

sponds with that which has been drawn since Goethe, more broadly and often invidiously, between symbolism and allegory. The symbolic is the only possible expression of some essence, according to Yeats, whereas the allegorical may be one out of many. In the latter case, we are less engaged by the symbol itself than by what is arbitrarily symbolized. Yet when the fish is not a religious acrostic but Captain Ahab's whale, it is emblematic; and then, as W. H. Auden duly warns us, we must not expect a one-to-one correspondence. For what we then encounter is not an allegorical reference to something else in some particular respect, but a multiplicity of potential cross-references to other categories of experience.

These formulations could be tested by turning again to *Moby Dick* and applying the polysemous method, the fourfold scheme of interpretation that Dante invited his readers to follow, which extends the meaning beyond the literal to the three figurative levels: allegorical, moral, and anagogical. Later allegories may not be as multi-leveled as the *Divine Comedy*; it is hard to discern more than three planes in the *Faery Queene* or two in the *Pilgrim's Progress*. Under the subsequent impact of realism, the allegorical and the anagogical tend to wither away; the moral blends with the literal or drops out altogether as writers turn from the Celestial City to Vanity Fair. But the Middle Ages maintained the sharp differentiation formulated in a Latin distich which can be conveniently paraphrased: the literal tells us what happens, the allegorical what to believe, the moral what to do, and the anagogical whither to strive. Thus, literally *Moby*

*Dick* is concerned with the voyage of the Pequod, the subject of whaling, the science of cetology; allegorically with society on shipboard, the parable of Ahab's "irresistible dictatorship"; morally with a series of object-lessons, such examples as the monkey-rope, the ligature of brotherhood that binds Ishmael to Queequeg; and anagogically . . . *"Quo tendas?* whither art thou striving?"

That is the question, and Melville offers no categorical answer. Dante knew, or believed he knew, the object of his journey. No traveler, to be sure, had returned to map out the topography of the next world, but Dante's account was based on the *terra firma* of assumptions universally shared, while Melville put out to sea in lone pursuit of "the ungraspable phantom of life." He was enough of a transcendentalist to ponder the meaning of this "great allegory, the world," enough of an iconoclast to strike through the pasteboard mask of outer appearances, and enough of a skeptic to respect the uncharted mystery beyond it. But the anagoge, which for Dante is the fulfilment of providential design, for Melville remains an ultimate question mark. His overwhelming whale has been identified with—among other concepts—nature, fate, sex, property, the father-image, God Himself. It has meant various things to varying critics because it is Melville's enigma, like the doubloon nailed by Ahab to the mast, which signifies dollars to the Second Mate, the Zodiac to the First Mate, and the universe to the Captain. Shall we ever identify Moby Dick? Yes, when we have sprinkled salt on the tail of the Absolute, but not before.

In one of his prophetic moments Melville even anticipated atomic fission, describing the tail of the whale as if it were a cyclotron. "Could annihilation occur to matter," Ishmael exclaims, "this were the thing to do it." However, the atomic is just as far beyond our scope as the cosmic, and we cannot necessarily count upon the rock of dogma for that firm foundation on which Durandus constructed his medieval symbology. Are we then at the mercy of sheer subjectivity, of the irresponsible caprice of the overingenious critic, making symbols mean what he wants them to mean? Or have we still some criteria at our disposal, technical means for determining the relevance, if not the truth, of any given comment? Here I would venture to suggest that students of literature might profitably emulate the researches now being carried on in the plastic arts under the heading of Iconology. Some of us have been collecting images, but not interpreting them very satisfactorily; others have been tracing the history of ideas without paying much attention to formal context. Could we not hope for a discipline which would bring the tools of critical analysis to bear upon the materials of textual documentation, concentrating upon the thematic relationship between the idea and the image? Shall we ever discover the archetype behind them both except by comparative study of its most impressive manifestations?

This is more easily called for than provided. The leaders of the Iconological School are brilliantly conspicuous for their combination of discernment and learning. We shall not have literary iconologists in our departments of English until our discerners have

picked up a little learning and our learners have somehow acquired a little discernment. In the interim, are
there not a few reasonable game laws which we might
undertake to observe whenever we go fishing? Or,
to state the problem more pragmatically, could we
not agree upon a code of fair-trade practices which
might conduce to a closer meeting of critical minds?
Granted that divergence of opinion is salutary, indeed
necessary, for the evaluation of a work of art, and
that the very suggestiveness of some masterworks is
most richly attested by the variety of interpretations
accruing to them. Yet the work itself is always greater
than the sum of its interpretations, and unless these
are grounded within some frame of objective reference, we have no basis for differentiating between
perception and deception. After all, criticism, in a
Baconian phrase, is reason applied to imagination.
Doubtless the fourfold method of exegesis which
Dante appealed to and Saint Thomas propounded
would be somewhat hierarchical for our day. Nevertheless, in more democratic terms, the common consent of educated readers might be gained at four
descending levels of acceptance.

The first, which raises no questions, would be
strictly conventional. No one has any doubt what
Hawthorne intends by the accepted symbol of the
eagle over the door of the Custom-House in the in-
troductory chapter of *The Scarlet Letter*, and Melville's eagle soaring over the Catskills, though less
official, is a bird of the same feather. The second use
of the symbol is explicit, as when Melville glosses the
monkey-rope or moralizes up and down the deck in

*Moby Dick;* or, best of all, Hawthorne's scarlet letter itself—how similar in appearance, how different in connotation from the "crownèd A" of Chaucer's Prioress! Third, and here we cross an equatorial line, the implicit. "Thou too sail on, O ship of state!" is highly explicit, not to say conventional. But the good ship Pequod, like the frigate Neversink in *White-jacket, or The World in a Man o' War,* is a little world in itself, and when it goes down, what are we to make of the eagle that goes down with it or of that rather sinister emblem, the hand with a hammer? Melville's "Tartarus of Maids" is explicitly a humanitarian sketch of a New England factory and implicitly an obstetrical allegory of woman's fate. What is implied, in contrast to what is explained by the author himself, can be possibly gauged by what are known in Shakespearean commentary as "fervors" and "recurrences."

These are the patterns of repetition and emphasis, which in some fortunate cases can be reinforced by the facts of biography and the insights of psychology. Jay Leyda's *Melville Log* not only supplements the romances and tales, but fills in some missing segments of their imaginative configuration. Without such external evidence we could draw no sharp line between the implicit and, fourth, the conjectural level, or for that matter, between the conjectural and the inadmissable. But once we admit degrees of plausibility, we may entertain, for whatever enhancement it may be worth, any conjecture likely to enrich our apprehension of the part-and-parcel allegoricalness of the whole. Does it enrich our apprehension of the later novels of Henry James if we construe them as Swedenborgian allegories? There is one tangential fact in support of this argument: the Swedenborgianism of the elder Henry James. And that is outweighed by the clearest expressions of intention, as well as by the internal consistency of the author's habits of thinking and writing. Therefore the purported symbolism is not conventional nor explicit nor implicit; it is at best conjectural, and since it obscures rather more than it illuminates, it should probably be discarded as inadmissable. Let us look for figures in the carpets, and not in the clouds.

And let us return, for the last time, to the whale. Surely no other literary symbol has invited and evaded so much conjecture; surely Melville intended to keep us guessing up to the bitter end and afterward. His book does not resemble life the less because it leaves us in a state of suspense. But just as insecurity seeks authority, just as complexity seeks simplification, just as pluralism seeks unity, so our critics long for the archetypal because they are bedeviled by the ambiguous. Groping amid ambiguities, they become increasingly hot for certainties, and symbols, they desperately hope, will provide the keys. So every hero may seem to have a thousand faces, every heroine may be a white goddess *incognita*, and every fishing trip turns out to be another quest for the Holy Grail. However, that boy of Hemingway's fishing in Big Two-Hearted River is not a type but an individual. He is not Everyman, he is Nick Adams, and like every other single human being, he is unique. The river in which he fishes is neither the Nile nor the Liffey; it is a stream which runs through the Upper Peninsula of the state of Michigan. The sun that beats on his back is the same old planet that has generated myths since the world began, but the feeling it evokes is the existential conjunction of the scene, the moment, and human sensibility. Literature can give us many other things, but it gives us, first and last, a taste of reality.

# YEATS AND THE CARELESS MUSE

by

JOHN FREDERICK NIMS

T HE CARELESS MUSE: THE
poets, more often than not, have had
a kind word for disheveled beauty. When Herrick
admitted that sweet disorder, distraction, things er-
ring, neglectful, confused, tempestuous, careless, wild,
more bewitched him than when art was too precise
in every part, he was of course repeating a theme of
Ben Jonson's in the little song from *Epicoene*:

> Robes loosely flowing, hair as free:
> Such sweet neglect more taketh me
> Than all th' adulteries of art . . .

With Jonson we are on our way back to the classics,

to such passages as that of Ovid in the *Amores*, where
the poet admires as *neglecta decens* a girl still disheveled in the morning. Venus first appears to Aeneas
with tresses windblown: *dederatque comam diffundere
ventis*. It is not easy, in fact, to find the poet who
prefers a girl soignée. Better to clip the locks off entirely, so one can contemplate a bracelet of bright
hair about the bone, or calm hair meandering in pel-
lucid gold. Or so one can write a mock-heroic poem.
But until the glittering forfex snips the tresses, the
poet tends to admire them, with Keats, half lifted by
the winnowing wind, or he cries with Browning

> Dear dead women, with such hair, too—what's become
>   of all the gold
> Used to hang and brush their bosoms? . . .

or sings with Rossetti

> The hair that lay along her back
> Was yellow as ripe corn . . .

or with Hopkins: "loose locks, long locks, lovelocks
. . ." Even Milton, in his brief Prufrockian dream of
a *fête champêtre*, sees himself sporting with the "tan-
gles" of Neaera's hair, and his later Eve

> Her unadorned gold'n tresses wore
> Dissheveld . . .

So with the moderns. Wallace Stevens contrasts elaborate Oriental and English coiffeurs with the morning dishevelment of a girl *neglecta decens*:

> Alas! have all the barbers lived in vain
> That not one curl in nature has survived?
> Why, without pity on these studious ghosts
> Do you come dripping in your hair from sleep?

Robert Frost, who himself associates with a cunningly offhand muse, sees one of his loveliest if most disturbing visions of girlhood

> standing to the waist
> In goldenrod and brake,
> Her shining hair displaced . . .

Even Mr. Eliot grows lyrical here:

> Blown hair is sweet, brown hair over the mouth
>     blown,
> Lilacs and brown hair . . .

The one exception I think of is Ezra Pound, always fussy about hair arrangement. He likes it elegant, with formalized hair-dos "cut straight across [the] forehead," or piled up "on the left side of her headpiece . . .," or "done in small ringlets" or "strait" or "a basketwork of braids." Even when he translates εὐπλόκαμος he does up the hair and covers it: the girl that Homer said had nice curls now appears "trim-coifed." But the poets almost unanimously are for unbound tresses. None more than Yeats; in nearly half of the poems in *The Wind Among the Reeds* he mentions long hair loosened.

But we dawdle too long outside the beauty parlors of Parnassus. Which way, one may wonder, is poetry from here? We can return via Cicero; a passage in the *Orator* might be paraphrased as follows: A speaker [and surely a poet] should not seem too fastidious in putting words together; there is a *non ingrata neglegentia,* a certain carelessness not unattractive because it makes him seem first a human being and only then a man of eloquence, a kind of carelessness to be achieved only with great care. *Quaedam neglegentia est diligens.* Just as certain women are loveliest without jewels or elaborate curls, so this easy way of speaking pleases most when it seems that little or nothing has been done to improve it. *Neglegentia* is Cicero's word: Ben Jonson's "sweet neglect."

Why have the poets and their critics found this delight in disorder? Is it because disorder is more winning than composure? Horace still charms with graceful negligence, Pope reminds us: and by means of "brave disorder" we snatch a grace beyond the reach of art. Or is it because the poet, his mind on greater things, is above minutiae, realizing (again with Pope) that not to know some trifles is a praise? Or is it because disorder is closer to the spirit of nature, that *rerum concordia discors?* Ben Jonson, in his setting for *The Masque of Blackness,* seems to feel so: his machine-made waves imitate "that orderly disorder, which is common in nature." Or, finally, is it because disorder is a mark of emotion? Longinus says so—if indeed we need an authority to validate what we see around us. Placidity, he says, expresses itself in neat arrangement; emotion, however, in disorder: ἐν ἀταξίᾳ δὲ τὸ πάθος.

Here then are four suggestions as to why carelessness is dear to the poets: it is pleasing in itself, it is magnanimous, it is true to nature, and it is characteristic of passion. Particularly the last three account, though not completely, for the long alliance between Yeats and the careless muse.

## II

My title, of course, is from "Among School Children." Yeats is saying that even the greatest men at the time of their fame have become scarecrows: old coats upon old sticks to scare a bird. Plato, Aristotle, and

> World-famous golden-thighed Pythagoras
> Fingered upon a fiddle-stick or strings
> What a star sang and careless Muses heard . . .[1]

Careless muses—the adjective is curious. According to an older etymology the word *muse* grew from a root meaning *mind*. The derivation, even if discredited, suggests a popular interpretation: the muses are the mindful ones, the personification "of the highest intellectual and artistic aspirations"—anything, it would seem, but careless. For Chaucer, the muse was "mighty"; for Spenser, "lofty," "tender," or, especially, "mournful." In *Henry V* Shakespeare cries "O for a Muse of fire!" The poets disparage her too, as in a lovers' quarrel: for Donne she is "undiscerning"; for Milton "thankless"; for Wordsworth "niggardly" and "unchary," as in his case she sometimes was. But whatever her faults, she tends to be a hard-working lady; she "labors" with Iago in the throes of composition, as indeed she labors with the poets. There are few hand-outs from the muse.

Tennyson wrote of the "placid marble muses, looking peace." But Yeats found them quite different. "The Muses," he wrote in *A Vision*, "resemble women who creep out at night and give themselves to un-

[1] All quotations from the poetry of Yeats are from *The Collected Poems of W. B. Yeats* (New York: The Macmillan Company, 1956), reprinted by permission.

known sailors and return to talk of Chinese porcelain
. . . or the Ninth Symphony . . ." His own muse, he
was persuaded, grew younger as he grew older and
more rheumatic; but she came to have not the innocence of youth so much as its exuberance and its wild-
ness, the latter a quality Yeats thought inherent in the
creative personality. When criticized for not rising
for the national anthem, he wrote "There are only
three classes I respect, the aristocracy who are above
fear; the poor who are beneath it, and the artists
whom God has made reckless." The artist resembled
the human types that Yeats most admired: the horseman with his aristocratic nonchalance, the fisherman
with his indifference to the workaday world and its
interests, the beggar with his happy-go-lucky unconcern. The casual manner, in fact, became the very
touchstone of integrity:

> And call those works extravagance of breath
> That are not suited for such men as come
> Proud, open-eyed, and laughing to the tomb.

Of course literature has always had its great disdain-
ers: Dante's Farinata, up to his waist in the fire he
scorns, is possibly the most memorable. Many an
Elizabethan, on and off the stage, died like the Thane
of Cawdor:

> As one that had been studied in his death,
> To throw away the dearest thing he owed,
> As 'twere a careless trifle.

If the heroes of Yeats seem less studied than im-
pulsive, it may be because their creator professed to
disdain the way of logic. His *Autobiography* tells how

he hated (though he admired) the "logical straightness" of Shaw: it was not the crooked way of life.
Presently he had "a nightmare that [he] was haunted
by a sewing machine, that clicked and shone . . ." For
Yeats, there was more insight in fervor than in logic:

> A passion-driven exultant man sings out
> Sentences that he has never thought . . .

Thought in the mind, that is, for there was also a
thinking of the whole body, a thinking in a marrow-
bone. The mere brain-thinker is a half man; his partial
mind has to be completed by passions of the flesh and
blood. This is probably best put in "Michael Robartes
and the Dancer," which lectures a young girl on the un-
importance of mind compared with physical beauty:

> But bear in mind your lover's wage
> Is what your looking glass can show.

When she protests, she is told that women can be
happy, and make men happy, only on condition that
they

> banish every thought, unless
> The lineaments that please their view
> When the long looking glass is full
> Even from the footsole think it too.

To which the puzzled girl can only reply: "They say
such different things at school." The muse too should
seem not to take thought, thought which only "in-
creases unreality."

> Thought is a garment and the soul's a bride
> That cannot in that trash and tinsel hide.

Whatever may be obscure in the cones and gyres and
wheels and spheres of *A Vision* (that true Coney Island of the mind), certain things are clear. Of the

twenty-eight incarnations or phases of the moon,
Phase 15, that of the full moon, is the phase of complete beauty—and surely the most careless phase. Care
means thought and effort, but even as we approach
Phase 15 "thought is disappearing into image; and in
Keats, in some ways the perfect type, intellectual
curiosity is at its weakest . . ." The historical period
that corresponds to this phase is that of the Italian
Renaissance between 1450 and 1550. Yeats particularly mentions Botticelli, Da Vinci, Mantegna. Now
Mantegna and the Quattrocento are evoked in an impressive poem, "Her Vision in the Wood," in which
we have an image of thoughtless thought, a procession
of something like the careless muses.

> Dry timber under that rich foliage,
> At wine-dark midnight in the sacred wood,
> Too old for a man's love I stood in rage
> Imagining men. Imagining that I could
> A greater with a lesser pang assuage
> Or but to find if withered vein ran blood,
> I tore my body that its wine might cover
> Whatever could recall the lip of lover.
>
> And after that I held my fingers up,
> Stared at the wine-dark nail, or dark that ran
> Down every withered finger from the top;
> But the dark changed to red, and torches shone,
> And deafening music shook the leaves; a troop
> Shouldered a litter with a wounded man,
> Or smote upon the string and to the sound
> Sang of the beast that gave the fatal wound.
>
> All stately women moving to a song
> With loosened hair or foreheads grief-distraught,
> It seemed a Quattrocento painter's throng,

A thoughtless image of Mantegna's thought—
Why should they think that are for ever young?
Till suddenly in grief's contagion caught,
I stared upon his blood-bedabbled breast
And sang my malediction with the rest.

That thing all blood and mire, that beast-torn wreck,
Half turned and fixed a glazing eye on mine,
And, though love's bitter-sweet had all come back,
Those bodies from a picture or a coin
Nor saw my body fall nor heard it shriek,
Nor knew, drunken with singing as with wine,
That they had brought no fabulous symbol there
But my heart's victim and its torturer.[2]

What interests us now is the third stanza, and especially its fifth line. The muse, as Yeats remembered when he was given the Nobel Prize, is young, and because young need not think. She is careless—as here the stately women, so lost in the intoxication of their singing, seem blind to the agony in their midst. "Why should they think that are for ever young?" In a passage of *A Vision*, written about the same time as the poem, Yeats contrasts the "never-ceasing care" of statues of Roman senators with the ease of Greek sculptures. "Those riders upon the Parthenon had all the world's power in their moving bodies, and in a movement that seemed, so were the hearts of man and beast set upon it, that of a dance . . . What need had those young lads for careful eyes?" Here is the same question in the same form, even in the same rhythm, though one is in prose. Thoughtlessness is proper to youth and to the phase of perfect beauty.

[2] "Her Vision in the Wood," copyright 1933, revised 1961, by Bertha Georgie Yeats.

### III

But when did Yeats take up with the careless muse?
Not certainly in his earliest work, in which passion,
so fierce and vibrant later, is neurasthenic, careworn.
*Restless, sick, dreary, weary, fretful, pale, grey, dim,
waning, mournful*—these were among his favorite
words at the time. More than once the human child
is urged to come away from a world more full of
weeping than he can understand. The muse of the
soggy handkerchief saw several volumes through the
press; it was not until *In the Seven Woods* (1904),
published when Yeats was almost forty, that there are
signs of a break with her. He begins to cut himself
short when the complaints grow lengthy:

>                     but enough,
> For when we have blamed the wind we can blame love.

And in "Adam's Curse" he expresses a paradox we
will see again and again in the later poems: proper
carelessness (as Cicero had observed) is a kind of
care, and the verse of the careless muse, like the
beauty of a woman, is the result of much hard work
done privately.

>     A line will take us hours maybe;
> Yet if it does not seem a moment's thought,
> Our stitching and unstitching has been naught . . .

Six years later in *The Green Helmet*, his trifling with
the casual muse has become serious indeed; he is almost committed to the baggage. The tone of mockery
is quite new; the form it takes is disdain of the popu-
lace and popular taste, indifference to any event, pro-

vided the soul maintain its integrity. If it does, he asks defiantly, "Why should I be dismayed?" Hardly a question he would have asked earlier, with reasons for dismay on every side. But now he begins to profess indifference toward much that had troubled him before: toward love, toward politics, and even toward his own work. He begins to have words of praise for Dionysius. Laughter is heard for the first time in the world of his poetry—laughter that would have been so out of place in the misty air of the earlier work, except for the fey, unearthly laughter of the Sidhe. And he was coming to a new conception of language, as "wrought of high laughter, loveliness and ease"—exactly the tone of the careless muse. The poem in which this line occurs, made up of three questions and nothing else, is typical of the casual new style: no statement, no commitment. Up to now there had not been much questioning in his poetry, but suddenly the laurel wreath is fairly hooked together with interrogation marks. "No Second Troy," for example, is made up of nothing but four questions. Of the twenty-one poems in this collection, exactly one third end with a question mark, whereas only two or three poems of the hundred published before had done so.

Another negligence first shown at this time is a forgetting, or rather a not bothering to remember, this or that. Yeats also begins to use various phrases of indifference, like impatient gestures sweeping aside details: "Let all that be . . ."; "What matter . . . ?" "Enough if . . ."

And into this book his first horseman comes galloping—that figure of the reckless and noble rider who is the opposite of merchant and clerk. We will hear the thunder of those arrogant hooves often throughout the greater poems, and when the curtains are finally drawn on the great drama of Yeats' passion, they will close upon a horseman against the sky.

## IV

Why then, when Yeats was about forty-five, did his poetry take on a new life, a reckless life of arrogance and disdain, of laughter at times derisive, at times exultant? Circumstances that might have broken a man less tough had much to do with the change. In 1903 he heard that the woman he had loved in vain for nearly twenty years had made an unworthy marriage. During the next five or six years he wrote only one lyric; "his fists," says one of his critics, "were tightly clenched."

Disillusioned too by public events in Ireland, he remembered Goethe on Irish jealousy: "The Irish seem to me like a pack of hounds, always dragging down some noble stag." Three times Yeats was in at the death of such a stag, and he never forgot. When, in his twenties, he saw the destruction of Parnell, he had no style capable of dealing with the "dramatic exit of the heaven-born leader"; he wrote only a bad poem whose title, complete with dash and exclamation mark, was "Mourn—And Then Onward!" But the theme of the proud hero dragged to ruin for a woman's sake recurs in his work, to culminate in the strange and violent "Parnell's Funeral" of forty years later.

In 1907 he raged again at the Irish, who had rioted against *The Playboy of the Western World.* Two years later Synge was dead. Not long after, the third blow came when Lady Gregory's nephew offered his great collection of French Impressionists to the city of Dublin provided it would build a suitable museum —and the city refused. The people, it seemed, did not want great leadership, did not want great drama, did not want great art—and for each of these rejections Yeats lashed out with a savagery that settled at last into contempt. More and more he expressed indifference toward what most people thought, toward his own past efforts, and finally even indifference toward his own indifference:

> We too had many pretty toys when young:
> A law indifferent to praise or blame . . .

## V

But the gestures of disdain had a theoretical sanction as well: they followed from Yeats' theory of the very nature of reality. The phenomenal world symbolized in *A Vision* is irrational because it is a series of unresolved antinomies. The only sound attitude to take toward it is a certain detachment, a certain indifference—or since, for Yeats, perfection exists in the interaction of opposites, a certain indifference together with a passionate concern. More about these opposites later; enough for now to note that his carelessness has a metaphysical or existential character.

Facts that account then for Yeats' new air of carelessness are not far to seek. But since he was a traditionalist who loved "precedents out of beautiful old books," he must have been pleased to find his own theories sustained by, though probably not originating in, Baldesar Castiglione's *The Book of the Courtier*. In *The Bounty of Sweden* Yeats tells how his "memory had gone back twenty years to that summer when a friend [Lady Gregory] read out to me at the end of each day's work Castiglione's commendations and descriptions of that court of Urbino, where youth for certain brief years imposed upon drowsy learning the discipline of its joy . . ." The summer would have been that of 1904; in 1907 Yeats visited Urbino. There are several longing references to it in his work, two of them in a diary of 1909. And in a poem that complains of the people, he wishes he might have

> climbed among the images of the past—
> The unperturbed and courtly images—
> Evening and morning, the steep street of Urbino
> To where the Duchess and her people talked
> The stately midnight through until they stood
> In their great window looking at the dawn . . .

The allusion, in which for us the important word is "unperturbed," is to the last page of *The Book of the Courtier*, a book that confirmed Yeats in his preference for a beneficent and responsible aristocratic life, and probably also brought into focus for him a something he had been working toward in his own art: the air of elegant unconcern. Two or three quotations will illustrate the kind of thing that must have struck him in Castiglione's book.

Having thought many times already about how this grace is acquired . . . I have found quite a universal rule which in this matter seems to me valid above all others, and in all human affairs whether in word or deed: and that is . . . to practice in all things a certain *sprezzatura* [nonchalance], so as to conceal all art and make whatever is done or said appear to be without effort and almost without any thought about it. [I, 26]

What eye is so blind as not to see . . . the grace of that cool *disinvoltura* [ease] . . . in many of the men and women here present, who seem in words, in laughter, in posture not to care; or seem to be thinking more of everything than of that, so as to cause all who are watching them to believe that they are almost incapable of making a mistake . . . ? [I, 26]

. . . . . . . . . . . . . . .

Consider how ungraceful that rider is who tries to sit so very stiff in his saddle . . . compared with one who appears to give no thought to the matter and sits his horse as free and easy as if he were on foot.[3] [I, 27]

In Castiglione, Yeats could have found many of his other preferences anticipated, but probably what most impressed him was the desirability, in art as in other things, of the nonchalance shown by those "who seem in words, in laughter, in posture not to care . . . ," and who thereby give the impression of supreme mastery. All this he has in mind in "Ego Dominus Tuus":

> We have lit upon the gentle, sensitive mind
> And lost the old nonchalance of the hand;
> Whether we have chosen chisel, pen, or brush,
> We are but critics, or but half create,
> Timid, entangled, empty and abashed . . .

In a letter to Dorothy Wellesley long afterwards

[3] From *The Book of the Courtier* by Baldesar Castiglione, translated by Charles Singleton. Copyright © 1959 by Charles S. Singleton and Edgar de N. Mayhew. Reprinted by permission of Doubleday & Company, Inc.

(May 22, 1936) he wrote: "Those little poems of
yours are nonchalant, & nonchalance is declared by
Castigleone [sic] essential to all true courtiers—so it
is to warty lads & poets."

## VI

Passion rather than thought, abandon rather than
prudence, defiance rather than conformity, the air of
nonchalance rather than any show of effort—from
about 1910 on, these were to be the preferences of the
careless muse. *Responsibilities,* Yeats' 1914 volume,
opens with what T. S. Eliot describes as "that violent
and terrible epistle dedicatory . . . more than half a
lifetime to arrive at this freedom of speech." Yeats,
recalling his ancestors, remembers especially his grand-
father's recklessness and what it taught him:

> Old merchant skipper that leaped overboard
> After a ragged hat in Biscay Bay;
> You most of all, silent and fierce old man,
> Because the daily spectacle that stirred
> My fancy, and set my boyish lips to say,
> 'Only the wasteful virtues earn the sun . . .'

Not caring about this or that is a major theme in the
book. "The Three Beggars," for example, is a fable
to show that men who least desire get most. In the
poem a king offers a thousand pounds to whichever
of the beggars can first fall asleep within three days.
They scheme and bicker, manage to do everything except that one thing they too much desire. The moral
is clear to an old crane who has been standing by:

> It's certain there are trout somewhere
> And maybe I shall take a trout
> If but I do not seem to care.

But with the mention of this ode to indifference, suppose we drop our book-by-book scrutiny for a broader survey of the later work.

"Because there is safety in derision . . . ," the safety of disengagement, Yeats often has recourse to it. One section of "1919" is all mockery: the first three stanzas in turn mock "the great," "the wise," and "the good," and in the fourth Yeats turns on himself: "Mock mockers after that." More than once he looks with derision on himself when young.

> When I was young
> I had not given a penny for a song
> Did not the poet sing it with such airs
> That one believed he had a sword upstairs . . .

and the later "The Circus Animals' Desertion" casts an even more disenchanted eye on the earlier preoccupations of his muse.

As she became younger, she also became more laughter-loving, though never, I think, comic. She may have learned to laugh from Castiglione's ideal of those who "seem in words, in laughter, in posture not to care," as she may have learned from him to desire, as the supreme achievement of a great house, a "written speech Wrought of high laughter, loveliness and ease." Yeatsian laughter: a joyous and whole-hearted acceptance of experience, of the worst it can offer, and particularly of death itself. His jaunty heroes "have lived in joy and laughed into the face of Death," as he says in "Upon a Dying Lady," surely one of the most undaunted of deathbed sequences. With such laughter, gay and terrible, a man meets his fate: in an exultant surrender of personality to the great vortex

of being, the spirit of the gyres. There is more of such
laughter in *Last Poems* than elsewhere; it rings out
even more strongly as the poet himself draws near to
death. As souls pass on the backs of dolphins to the
shores of another life, in "News for the Delphic
Oracle,"

> The ecstatic waters laugh because
> Their cries are sweet and strange . . .

In "Lapis Lazuli" there is gaiety in both the oriental
philosophers and the tragic heroes of the west.

Laughter, like song and the dance, is a carefree
Dionysian release quite beyond logic. So, preemi-
nently, is drunkenness, which comes in for its share
of praise. Drunkenness, that state of apparently
heightened nonrational perception and participation,
is for Yeats, as for some of the mystics, a metaphor
for blessedness. So too are various deprivations: blind-
ness, deafness, dumbness:

> Those men that in their writings are most wise,
> Own nothing but their blind stupified hearts.

Helen's poet, he never forgets, was a blind man.

Other Dionysian forces, antirational and imprudent
if hardly nonchalant, are extolled: lust (Hanrahan's
"horrible splendor of desire"), rage, folly, frenzy
(called sometimes "blind," sometimes "drunken"),
and indeed madness itself. For the wasteful virtues,
and much that Yeats most cherishes, are in the eyes of
the world a kind of madness—the literal and figurative
senses of the word run together. "All that delirium of
the brave": were the Irish heroes mad because they
gave their lives for their country as one might for love?

> You'd cry, 'Some woman's yellow hair
> Has maddened every mother's son':
> They weighed so lightly what they gave.

To this rapture of madness one is conducted by love, beauty, poetry, music, wine. Yeats writes of "eyes that beauty has driven mad," and poetry and alcohol have the same effect:

> And certain men, being maddened by those rhymes,
> Or else by toasting her a score of times . . .

Such considerations led him to say of his own art, "If I triumph I must make men mad." Such drunken madness is that of Crazy Jane, who really has a superior kind of knowledge, that of the deep-considering mind which has known much and looked into the very heart of things. Indeed, madness in this sense is the sum of human knowledge:

> I shudder and I sigh to think
> That even Cicero
> And many-minded Homer were
> *Mad as the mist and snow.*

Frenzy, fury, folly, madness—these are to be invoked rather than deplored. Yeats expresses the hope on one occasion that a beloved friend will be visited not by satisfied conscience but by "that great family . . . The Proud Furies each with her torch on high."

For what straightness, what sanity is possible in the world of "that dolphin-torn, that gong-tormented sea"? Yeats liked all crooked, zigzag, spinning things; he was fascinated by the "great labyrinth" of another's being. He liked gyres and spires and winding stairs— is perhaps the only reader who might have given the unexpected answer to George Herbert's, "Is all good structure in a winding stair?" In general he preferred vagrants to settled citizens; professed to admire all sorts of wild, purposeless activity: "an aimless joy is a pure joy."

Since true wisdom is "a something incompatible with life," it is not surprising that Yeats comes out frankly at times for ignorance: "all knowledge lost in trance Of sweeter ignorance." Hence he is careless about details, sometimes forgets or professes to forget, often with fine poetic effect:

> Hanrahan rose in frenzy there
> And followed up those baying creatures toward—
> O toward I have forgotten what—enough!

On one occasion, in speaking of the reckless horseman Robert Gregory, he matches the rider's deliberate indifference with an indifference of his own:

> At Mooneen he had leaped a place
> So perilous that half the astonished meet
> Had shut their eyes; and where was it
> He rode a race without a bit?

Forgetting: a dismissal of the unworthy, a kind of disdaining. In *Estrangement* Yeats recalls the night an Irish mob was rioting against Synge's *Playboy:* "No man of all literary Dublin dared show his face but my own father, who spoke to, or rather in the presence of, the howling mob with sweetness and simplicity. I fought them, he did a finer thing—forgot them."

The ethical counterpart of careless memory is indifference to past conduct; Yeats, who came to believe that the soul's "own sweet will is heaven's will," thought that only passionate moments should be preserved in that great storehouse of communal memories, the Anima Mundi. But remorse, as the beginning of judgment, is of the intellect and therefore suspect. Conscience too is a hindrance; if the great lover Hanrahan has ever failed to win a woman, he must blame "some silly over-subtle thought Or anything called conscience once"—the last word implying that Hanrahan has matured beyond conscience. To the heroic poets whose integrity he praises in "The Grey Rock" he says: "You . . . unrepenting faced your ends." And in old age he grieved, "Repentance keeps my heart impure."

## VII

And yet, to return to "Her Vision in the Wood": "A thoughtless image of Mantegna's thought." Beyond the thoughtless, always thought; beyond the careless, always care. Always the insistence on measure, precision, craftsmanship:

> Irish poets, learn your trade,
> Sing whatever is well made . . .

For the poet whose nonchalance we have been finding everywhere is at the same time one of the most earnest of craftsmen. This would have seemed no contradiction to Cicero, with his *neglegentia diligens*, and still less so to Yeats, who believed that a quality finds fulfillment in its opposite. Crazy Jane gives expression to one of his deepest convictions when she cries:

> Fair and foul are near of kin
> And fair needs foul . . .

Yeats was at once careful and careless, careful to seem careless; out of the tension between these opposites arise some of the finest effects of his art. In a little poem called "The Dawn" he speaks of "the careless planets in their courses"; careless, perhaps, but moving with mathematical precision, as Yeats himself did when he wrote. He once praised Lady Gregory's house as one in which "passion and precision have been one"; to a friend he insisted that "the very essence of genius, of whatever kind, is precision." And when H. J. C. Grierson sent Yeats his new edition of Donne, Yeats observed that "the more precise and learned the thought, the greater the beauty, the passion."

The effect of nonchalance was achieved with a labor that Yeats found "very great," as he tells us more than once. "Metrical composition is always very difficult to me, nothing is done upon the first day, not one rhyme is in its place, and when at last the rhymes begin to come, the first rough draft of a six-line stanza takes the whole day." And: "When I wrote verse, five or six lines in two or three laborious hours were a day's work, and I longed for somebody to interrupt me . . . " He wrote little or no free verse, preferring the tougher stanza forms, of which he worked in a great many. "Leda and the Swan," which so shocked his typist that, breaking into tears, she refused to copy it, is in that most respectable of forms, the sonnet. Carelessness, in short, is another of the famous masks; behind it always is the frown of the scrupulous muse.

This is no surprise if we remember what company the careless muses were keeping:

> World-famous golden-thighed Pythagoras
> Fingered upon a fiddle-stick or strings
> What a star sang and careless Muses heard . . .

Pythagoras: science no less than music. When Yeats quoted the whole stanza in a letter to Mrs. Shakespear (September 24, 1926), he said, "Pythagoras made some measurement of the intervals between notes on a stretched string." Stately Pythagoras, tall Pythagoras, who as passion and precision appears twice amid his choir of love in the poetry of Yeats, is intellect, calculation, number, measurement. This we see most memorably in that remarkable late poem, "The Statues." Much of Yeats' curious system supports the poem, but what it means, in brief, is that the scientific measurements of Pythagoras made possible the proportions of a sculpture and the expression of a beauty which the Greeks came to see in human beings; it was this spirit of precision and clarity rather than the Greek fleet which repulsed the Persian menace. The poet concludes by calling on the Pythagorean spirit to save Ireland from the confusion of modern values. Yet in "The Statues" the products of the Greek sculptors are called "calculations that look but casual flesh"—casual but calculated, as Castiglione's nonchalance comes from a care and effort cunningly concealed.

## VIII

How Yeats took care to seem careless in matters of technique is a rewarding study. In diction, obviously he worked from the literary to the colloquial and conversational, but these always at concert pitch. He would have agreed with the author of *On the Sublime* that "a low word often reveals much more than an ornamental one; it is recognized from our daily life, and the familiar is that much nearer to carrying conviction." What the critic said about certain passages in Greek would characterize some of Yeats' work: they "graze the limits of vulgar and uncultivated speech, but are not uncultured in their expressiveness." Yeats himself wrote: "In later years I learnt that occasional prosaic words gave the impression of an active man speaking . . . Here and there in correcting my early poems I have introduced [such] numbness and dullness . . . that all might seem, as it were, remembered with indifference, except some one vivid image." The colloquial, offhand tone is heard not only in the language of Crazy Jane and the wild old wicked man or in the apparent irrelevance of the refrains; even in some of his loftiest passages Yeats may seem to saunter carelessly close to the limits of vulgar speech.

Other effects are more subtle. In a typical lyric of Yeats, a number of obstacles are set up for the poet. Every line has its metrical obligations; it rhymes with the following line or the one after that; the lines generally move in units of four. But with what ease, with how strong and unbroken a stride, the long sinewy sentences, sometimes only one to a poem, take these hurdles!

Rhyme itself is handled more and more airily. Not for any lack of ear; in the earliest work, the rhymes are invariably purse and perfect, at times wearily so. The first poem of the *Collected Poems* has not a single oblique rhyme in its fifty-odd lines: *dead-fed-head, joy-toy, world-whirled*, etc. But in *Responsibilities* (1914) everything is different. In the twenty-two lines of the dedicatory epistle we find such rhymes as *four-poor, blood-stood, cast-crossed, board-stirred, man-sun, sake-book*. Six off-rhymes, some quite far off. The percentage is even higher in later poems. But the discords are used with skill: how numbly *book*, supposed to rhyme with *sake*, thuds down in

> Pardon that for a barren passion's sake,
> Although I have come close on forty-nine,
> I have no child, I have nothing but a book . . .

Far more expressive, this off-key rhyme on a crucial word, than full rhyme could have been. From the time of *Responsibilities* on, Yeats is cavalier with rhyme: always aware of it, he makes the perfunctory bow in its direction, but with no deference whatever. He is the master, rhyme the servant. (A curious footnote: until about 1904, nearly always the word *love* is rhymed perfectly, for the most part with *above*. But after his own love had been embittered, the rhymes on *love* are habitually off-rhymes: *stuff, strove, off, enough*, though the *love-enough* rhyme is never used in the sense that there is or has been enough love.)

Yeats may have been confirmed in his later preference for off-rhyme by some remarks of Giuliano in *The Book of the Courtier*: ". . . in music . . . it is a great mistake to place two perfect consonances one after the other, for our sense of hearing abhors this, whereas it often enjoys a second or a seventh which in itself is a harsh and unbearable discord. And this is due to the fact that to continue in perfect consonances generates satiety and gives evidence of a too affected harmony . . ." (I, 28)

A studied nonchalance is apparent too in the handling of rhythm. From the beginning Yeats had a mastery of traditional effects and sometimes improved on them, as in "The Lake Isle of Innisfree" (published in 1890), with the suppression of a syllable energizing the fourth foot of the fourteeners, or as in " He Remembers Forgotten Beauty" (of five or six years later):

> When my arms wrap you round I press
> My heart upon the loveliness
> That has long faded from the world . . .

If we remember that this is basically the same meter as that of so many singsong little iambic tetrameters, we can appreciate a rhythm brilliantly expressive: in the first line the stringent spondees that make this perhaps the firmest embrace in poetry; the skipped beat of excitement in the second line; the spondee of extent of time in *long fade*, followed by the pyrrhic drop-off that further distances the *world*. Yeats permits himself no liberty in number of feet, but every liberty in their management. Freely as the stresses are handled, there is always discipline beneath the freedom: every line is unmistakably a four-stress line. He is not often as irregular as in the last line of "The Second Coming": "Slouches toward Bethlehem to be born." This carries the disintegration of the iambic

pentameter about as far as it can go without leaving
the ruins unrecognizable. But even here the apparently
haphazard rhythm is built on a careful meter, whether
one takes the line as headless with a pyrrhic in the
fourth foot or resolves it in one of the other possible
ways. A striking example of the jaunty but expressive
rhythm overriding the rigid meter is "The Fisherman,"
published in 1916. The poem employs a three-stress
iambic line, and yet out of its forty lines only three
are regular. Of all the variations, only once does the
same combination occur in two lines running. Yet
high-handed as the treatment of meter is, the variations are meaningful. A healthy rhythm, like the heart,
has its reasons for quickening or lagging—unlike a
metronone, whose rhythm never changes, blow it
kisses or look daggers.

Nearly always Yeats works in fixed stanza forms,
or he carries couplets or an *abab* pattern quite through
a poem. But at times, with what may seem negligence,
he drops a line. This can be exciting to those who
care about the trifles from which, as Michelangelo is
supposed to have said, comes the perfection which is
no trifle. Take as simple a poem as the early "The
Lover Mourns For the Loss of Love" (1898):

> Pale brows, still hands and dim hair,
> I had a beautiful friend
> And dreamed that the old despair
> Would end in love in the end:
> She looked in my heart one day
> And saw your image was there;
> She has gone weeping away.[4]

---

[4] "The Lover Mourns for the Loss of Love," copyright 1906,
revised 1934, by William Butler Yeats.

The first four lines are a common *abab* quatrain; the next three lines take us through three-fourths of another quatrain—and leave us there, our expectation vaguely unsatisfied, waiting for something, curtailed of the expected resolution which in our reading of thousands of quatrains had never failed us. But the poem is about loss; even in its form it suffers the bereavement. By its form as much as by the words, and far more subtly, it dramatizes that bereavement. But, with a calculation even about trifles, the line that might have been left unrhymed is given a rhyme from the preceding quatrain.

Another example: in "The Grey Rock" (1913), for one hundred and twelve lines the ear has been habituated to *abab: trade-cheese-remade-please, fashion-breath-passion-death.* Then, when the expectation is firmly grounded, we come upon:

> The bitter sweetness of false faces?
> Why must the lasting love what passes?
> Why are the gods by men betrayed?

First the sour rhymes of *faces-passes,* an unexpected couplet. Between them should have been the rhyme for *betrayed,* but *betrayed* hangs there forever without its rhyme, as if vibrant in a great silence. Then, having brought off his coup, the poet goes back to *up-sound-cup-ground.*

## IX

Once he had made the acquaintance of the careless muse, Yeats was faithful to the end. She is nowhere more present than in the eleven-line finale of his last poem, written only a few months before his death.

> Under bare Ben Bulben's head
> In Drumcliff churchyard Yeats is laid.
> An ancestor was rector there
> Long years ago, a church stands near,
> By the road an ancient cross.
> No marble, no conventional phrase;
> On limestone quarried near the spot
> By his command these words are cut:
>
> > *Cast a cold eye*
> > *On life, on death.*
> > *Horseman, pass by!*

The first five lines are offhand, almost brusque: merely "an ancestor," "a church," though we know that Yeats was fiercely proud of his ancestors and cherished the details of their history. The directions about the burial have the tone of indifference, impatience, as if he cared nothing for conventional pomp and wanted as little as possible done. And yet he gives a firm command: it must be *this* kind of stone, *these* words exactly. The final image of the horseman is all indifference, detachment, aloofness—or rather, the deliberate air of these. For, as Frank O'Connor has said, Yeats was no detached observer of life. He was an impassioned participant, but the air of nonchalance is what his muse demanded. Here every rhyme except the very last is cavalier, an arrant off-rhyme. Yeats omitted an original "Draw rein, draw breath" that preceded the last three lines and would have made them a symmetrical quatrain. Whether or not there is significance in the fact that *death* is not even deigned

its rhyme, there is surely significance in the choice
of a last word that resolves the series of dissonant
rhymes in a perfect harmony. As poetry this epitaph
would have pleased the careless muse, but we cannot
forget that Pythagoras too had a hand in it.

The poets, we said near the beginning of these ob-
servations, take delight in disorder because it is charm-
ing in itself, contemptuous of minutiae, true to nature, and eloquent of emotion. After his earliest poems
Yeats was less interested in charm for its own sake. But
high-handed and passionate he always was; more and
more he came to believe in a universe at loggerheads
with itself. He had other reasons too for august indifference: he had lost a sweetheart, though he had
found a book; he had left a country, though he had
sailed the seas; he had turned, like those giants of the
past, into old clothes upon old sticks to scare a bird.
But at least he had heard the careless planets singing
and seen the heaven disheveled:

> I dreamed as in my bed I lay,
> All night's fabulous wisdom come,
> That I had shorn my locks away
> And laid them on Love's lettered tomb:
> But something bore them out of sight
> In a great tumult of the air,
> And after nailed upon the night
> Berenice's burning hair.[5]

[5] Copyright 1933, revised 1961, by Bertha Georgie Yeats.

# THE ASPIRING CLOWN

by

R. W. B. LEWIS

ABOUT NO POEM BEFORE "Faustus and Helen" did Hart Crane have as much to say in his letters as "Chaplinesque," and no work satisfied him more. It was written over a relatively few days in early October 1921; on Christmas Day, when Crane heard from Gorham Munson that it had been published in the Paris-based magazine *Gargoyle*, he expressed an almost ceremonial gratification. "Your letter provided me with rich materials for a kind of Christmas tree, at least as thrilling as any of remotest childhood memories," he wrote. "Names and presences glitter and fascinate with all kinds of exotic suggestions on the branches. I can be grateful to you for the best of Christmas donations." Crane had more cause to celebrate than he guessed, for in perspective "Chaplinesque" encompasses more and holds a far more richly varied interest than Crane could possibly have known.

It is, for one thing, an even better poem in itself than Crane appreciated, or than his puzzled friends could make out. It is the most *finished* of all the early poems that depict the posture or status of the poet in the modern American scene; it brings to fruition aspects of this theme—so obsessive for the early Crane —that elsewhere, for example in "Black Tambourine" and "Porphyro in Akron," remain either congested or diffused, and in either case only partly realized. The poem is a fine product because it issues from still greater depths of what I call Crane's archetypal imagination, his creative intuition of the great recurring images through which poetry has always made its determining statements about human life. The archetype in the present instance is that of the clown: that is, of the poet as clown, or more exactly, as I shall want to suggest, of the poet, perhaps of Everyman, as Fool. This figure has a long and shifting history, some of which I shall want to glance at in order to press my claim for "Chaplinesque," but very little of which was in fact known to Crane. At the same time, in thus presenting his poetic self as a clown of sorts Crane voiced part of the essential mood of his literary epoch. Better: "Chaplinesque" did as much as any one short poem can do to establish a mood, and the subsequent projections of the artist as comedian, by Stevens, by cummings, later yet by Nathaniel West and Henry Miller, tend to thicken an image and an atmosphere introduced in their generation by Hart Crane. Finally, "Chaplinesque" warrants special attention among the writings of Crane's first phase just because, on one level, it is a product of the comic spirit.

It is also a product of the rueful spirit; it marks the moment of Jules Laforgue's most pervasive influence, and of Eliot's: the moment when Crane was most tempted towards the tone of witty and ironic self-derision. Crane's journey close to and his instinctive evasion of that particular shoal is a significant part of his story. His comic sense was an oddly compounded one, but it contained too large a fund of sheer high spirits to be seriously deflected by the Laforguian kind of irony; this, too, must be emphasized, in view of the long-standing and essentially misleading clichés about a tragic, wasted, and bedeviled life.

"Chaplinesque" was written soon after Crane had been enthralled by Charlie Chaplin's film, *The Kid*. He announced at once to Munson that "comedy has never reached a higher level in this country before," and that Chaplin was "a dramatic genius" of "the fabulous sort." Despite such stated enthusiasm and despite the poem's title (Crane's titles were not always so helpful or so cogent), the first readers quite failed, as Crane said, to " 'get' [his] idiom" in it. This must have cost him a grimace or two, for he was sure that in "Chaplinesque" he had hit closer to his own idiom than ever before; while the necessary elusiveness of the poet in the contemporary world was the poem's

very subject—that, and the hidden, tenuous rewards
of the poetic life.

> We make our meek adjustments,
> Contented with such random consolations
> As the wind deposits
> In slithered and too ample pockets.

To one correspondent, who was apparently unable
to identify the voice speaking in those lines, Crane
explained carefully that he had been "moved to put
Chaplin with the poets [of today]; hence the 'we' ";
in *The Kid*, he added, Chaplin had "made me feel
myself, as a poet . . . 'in the same boat' with him." The
comedian's film gesture thus becomes a metaphor of
the poet's shy strategy:

> For we can still love the world, who find
> A famished kitten on the step, and know
> Recesses for it from the fury of the street,
> Or warm torn elbow coverts.

That passage and the one which immediately follows
were paraphrased by Crane in a dogged but note-
worthy account to his friend William Wright: "Poetry, the human feelings, 'the kitten,' is so crowded
out of the humdrum, rushing, mechanical scramble of
today that the man who would preserve them must
duck and camouflage for dear life to keep them or
keep himself from annihilation."[1]

The very poetry ducks and camouflages, hugging its

[1] To Munson (in a letter of October 6, 1921), Crane related
"the symbol of the kitten" to that " 'infinitely gentle, infinitely
suffering thing' of Eliot's." The allusion is to Eliot's *Preludes*,
where "some infinitely gentle/Infinitely suffering thing" curls like
a kitten around "the thousand sordid images" of a dying epoch.

vulnerable tenderness to itself, as the poem continues:

We will sidestep and to the final smirk
Dally the doom of that inevitable thumb
That slowly chafes its puckered index toward us,
Facing the dull squint with what innocence
And what surprise!

With almost any of Charlie Chaplin's films in mind, we can immediately assign the "inevitable thumb" to the city cop who looms up so persistently, hand upraised, to block the little tramp, though Charlie manages to skip or sidestep past him for a while with an ingratiating smirk. But when the digital allusion leads from "thumb" to "index," another kind of prohibition enters the poem, the kind a poet has to dally or sidestep: the prohibition of, or turning thumbs down upon, the publication and the reading of certain books, as in the Catholic Index.[2] The figure of the poet, the would-be producer of books in modern America, is the alter ego of the slippery, impoverished, and obscurely outlaw tramp. The poet, too, must seek refuge for his insufficiently nourished sensibility from the fury of contemporary life. He must protect his small creations from the "dull squint" of a suspicious and forbidding public; and to that end, must invent poetic ways to sneak and slide around the obstacles to creative activity. He may, for instance, wear in his verses a disarming smirk and air of innocence, as though to assure the philistine reader that he, the poet, is neither serious nor dangerous. "Chaplinesque" is wreathed in

[2] Censorship was on Crane's mind. He was outraged at the reported censorship of *The Kid*. "What they could possibly have objected to, I cannot imagine. It must have been some superstition aroused by good acting."

just such a smirk, for it is not only an example of ironic self-deprecation, it is a defense of it, and of the poet's need to have recourse to its protection.

"And yet," Crane insists,

> And yet these fine collapses are not lies
> More than the pirouettes of any pliant cane;
> Our obsequies are, in a way, no enterprise.

If, like many of his literary ancestors and especially like Herman Melville, Crane was aware of the falsehoods into which cultural circumstance, as well as the very nature of poetic discourse, might seem to force a poet, he nonetheless affirms that the tactic of verbal trickery and the pose of self-abasement ("these fine collapses") only conceal, and do not violate, the truth perceived. Crane's affirmation is a characteristic effort to evade even the image of ironic evasion, and the subsequent word "obsequies" represents that effort in its most compressed form.

Over this word we may instructively linger. "Obsequies" has come to mean funeral rites, and given Crane's reference to "annihilation" in the letter quoted above, one might easily suppose that "Chaplinesque" is ultimately a poem about death: that the doom the poet-clown seeks to postpone is nothing other than death itself; and that the inevitable thumb, the puckered index, and the dull squint add up to a grim portrait of death personified. On the other hand, one might no less easily suppose that what Crane really meant was "obsequiousness," and that "obsequies" is simply an example of a muddled and ignorant use of language. But it is always a sounder policy with Crane

to assume that he knew what he was doing in his
selection of words; his poetry is a singularly dangerous
trap for the critically proud or unwary. In the present case, such muddle as there is comes from medieval
Latin, and Crane has not repeated it, he has cunningly
exploited it.[3] The original Latin word *obsequium*
meant servile compliance, but that meaning eventually
got confused with the word *exsequiae*, which does
refer to funeral ceremonies. Out of these two initially
quite unrelated Latin sources, Crane drew a word
with a packed and paradoxical significance. Part of
the poem's context, from "meek adjustments" through
"smirk" to "fine collapses," serves to reinvest "obsequies" with its etymological meaning of obsequiousness; another part, "the doom" and "the inevitable
thumb," gives it its familiar contemporary sense of
death and burial. In a single word, under intense con-
textual pressure, Crane thus says or suggests that the
self-demeaning compliance the contemporary world
demands of the poet or of any sensitive being would,
if submitted to, lead only to utter spiritual death.

But this is not the poet's enterprise, neither compliance nor death. His true enterprise is revealed in
the final passage of "Chaplinesque," when the enforced smirk of daytime experience becomes moon-
changed into a kind of holy laughter:

[3] Crane's Latin was small, but it existed. He studied it in school
and returned to it periodically thereafter; that is, he returned to
Latin poetry, Catullus especially and perhaps Virgil; Seneca is
quoted at the head of "Ave Maria" in *The Bridge*. Authoritative
evidence about his careful study of individual Latin words—
*obsequium*, for example—is lacking either way; the Latin-English
dictionary he is known to have possessed is not among his surviv-
ing books.

> The game enforces smirks; but we have seen
> The moon in lonely alleys make
> A grail of laughter of an empty ash-can,
> And through all sounds of gaiety and quest
> Have heard a kitten in the wilderness.

Again, a physical image inspired by Chaplin sym-
bolizes a poetic experience: an experience of beauty
that is implicitly religious, or, at least, chivalric in
nature. Crane knew that both Chaplin and his poem
about Chaplin might appear to some to be sentimental:
"Chaplin may be a sentimentalist, after all," he agreed,
(in another letter to Munson), "but he carries the
theme with such power and universal portent that
sentimentality is made to transcend itself into a new
kind of tragedy, eccentric, homely and yet brilliant."
This was the mode of transcendence Crane aimed at
in his closing lines, and which, in my view, he
achieved: in a hauntingly melodic vision of the
moon transforming a slum-alley ash-can into a silver
chalice— of the visionary imagination seeing in the
jungle of the actual a vessel of supernal beauty.

But such a moment is as rare as it is precious; the
main burden of "Chaplinesque" is still the image of
the poet as a shabby and antic tramp, a meek-faced
comedian on the run. This was the culmination (poetically speaking it was the perfection) of a series of
prior images by which Crane had advanced towards
artistic maturity by assessing the value of art itself in
the face of a derisive, indifferent, or bluntly hostile
world, and by appraising his own performance. In
the interesting mish-mash, "Porphyro in Akron"
(Winter 1920), he had made his point in a manner

flagrantly reminiscent of Eliot by juxtaposing present ugliness with past beauty, the actualities of Akron ("a shift of rubber workers" pressing down South Main Street at dawn, townspeople "using the latest ice-box and buying Fords") and the story of Porphyro, who steals in "with heart on fire" to awaken and escape with the maid Madeline in Keats's "The Eve of St. Agnes." The original Porphyro succeeded valiantly, despite a horde of "hyena foemen and hot-blooded lords"; but the contemporary Porphyro, who is reading "The Eve of St. Agnes" nostalgically in his hotel room, is ignominiously defeated by a noisy, materialistic, and utterly uninterested citizenry. In Akron, Porphyro-Crane reads aloud Keats's image of the moon and its magical effects:

> Full on this casement shown the wintry moon,
> And threw warm gules on Madeline's fair breast,
> As down she knelt for heaven's grace and boon . . .

But he is denied the moon; and his longing to awaken his own fair Madeline, the spirit of poetry itself, seems, under the circumstances, merely ludicrous:

> But look up, Porphyro—your toes
> Are ridiculously tapping
> The spindles at the foot of the bed.
> The stars are drowned in slow rain,
> And a hash of noises is slung up
>         from the street.
> You ought, really, to try to sleep,
> Even though, in this town, poetry's a
> Bedroom occupation.

Thus, Crane felt, was the contemporary poet made to look absurd by a hash-slinging environment. In

"My Grandmother's Love Letters" his best creative efforts were attended by slow rain, the rain that does not so much echo an oppressive world as comment upon his own creative inadequacy, with its "sound of gently pitying laughter." It is the kind of wordlessly sardonic comment the crematory clock would offer in "Praise for an Urn," "touching," as it does, "upon our praise/ Of glories proper to the time." The image in "Black Tambourine" had been a good deal more brutal. There the poet had been associated with the Negro, and, like the Negro, treated alternately as a subservient, tambourine-playing entertainer and as a sort of animal. But probably the most succinct and probing identification of his poetic self before "Chaplinesque" was contained in these lines:

> "The everlasting eyes of Pierrot
> And of Gargantua—the laughter."

The face so composed of contrasting comic traditions was of course a mask of sorts, a protection against further indignities, and "Chaplinesque" gives final articulation to the poet's felt need to adopt just that face of comedy. But Crane's comic sense was natural enough, and it constituted a more sizable portion of his temper than is sometimes acknowledged. His efforts to be explicitly funny in verse were usually almost embarrassingly bad, but he possessed another quality of humor, a tough and toughening amusement which did not spare the so-called dilemma of the modern writer. He was fully aware that there was something preposterous as well as painful in the situation; and something preposterous, too, in the general condition of man amid "the rushing, mechanical scramble of today." He had a ready perception of the lunatic aspect of human conduct and sometimes gave voice to it in the most athletic of obscenities. At such moments he saw himself belonging in good part to the commic tradition of bawdiness and gusto, of writers like Petronius, Rabelais, Cervantes, and Mark Twain, whom he had been reading with great relish (especially in 1919) and whom he named in a letter telling Gorham Munson that the latter was "too damned serious."

Humor is the artist's only weapon against the proletariat. Mark Twain knew thus, and used it effectively enough, take *1601* for example. Mencken knows it too. And so did Rabelais. . . . The modern artist has got to harden himself, and the walls of an ivory tower are too delicate and brittle a coat of mail for substitute. . . . I pray for both of us,—let us be keen and humorous scientists. And I would rather act my little tragedy without tears, although I would insist upon a tortured countenance and all sleekness pared off the muscles.

Crane, it is not too much to say, passed his apprenticeship not only by writing poems about poetry, as young men have always done, but by refining his own specific if complex feeling that the entire poetic enterprise was in one perspective ludicrous to the point of being clownish, and in another serious to the point of being sacred. He came into his own when he was able to see himself, and perhaps any other modern poet, as "a clown perhaps, but an aspiring clown"— a description registered in "Chaplinesque" a year before the poem in which those phrases actually occur,

Stevens's "The Comedian as the Letter C." The nature
of the achievement is indicated, even explained, by
some of the mingling contradictions just observed:
the "fine collapses" and the "grail of laughter" in
"Chaplinesque"; Pierrot's eyes and Gargantua's laughter; the "humorous scientists" (in the letter above)
and the "tortured countenance"; clownishness and
aspiration. The presence of these fertile contradictions
in Crane's mind and imagination, in his letters and in
his poetry, show how remarkably Crane, though only
half-knowingly, had come into tune with one of the
major traditions of Europe from what he regarded as
a provincial hinterland.

## II

The pirouetting clown in "Chaplinesque" is taken
first, of course, from the little tramp invented by the
Anglo-American comedian, Charlie Chaplin. But in
the range of his wistful aspiration and in the mythic
overtones of the final stanza (with its hint of the grail-
quest), he is also the figure revered in France as Charlot—a personality saluted in French writing many
times before "Chaplinesque," and twice by the surrealist poet Louis Aragon; a *persona*, a myth incarnate, a great illumination of the age and (as someone
said) the creator of "a sublime beauty, a new laughter."[4] This was not exactly Charlie Chaplin, it was a
Gallic enlargement of him; the screen image of Chap-

[4] Cf. Glauco Viazzi, *Chaplin e la critica* (Bari, Italy, 1955). Even
Signor Viazzi's enormously detailed check-list of poems, articles,
essays, and books about Chaplin in many countries and languages
is not complete. The discussion of Chaplin in Europe and America
was one of the cultural phenomena of the twenties and thirties,
and perhaps no single volume could appraise all of it.

lin underwent a great extension in the Parisian imagination. The French identified Charlot by grafting a native comic tradition to the original character. Both Charlot and the native tradition were made known to Crane in letters from abroad.[5]

The tradition was that of the clown known most recently in France as Pierrot. Chief among the literary contributions to that tradition had been the twenty-three "Pierrot poems" in a volume of verse called *L'Imitation de Notre Dame La Lune*, published in 1886, the year before his death, by the then twenty-six-year-old-poet, Jules Laforgue. The lines converge. In the fall of 1920, Crane acquired from Paris volumes of the poetry of Laforgue, Arthur Rimbaud, and Charles Vildrac. During the following summer and with help from more expert linguists, Crane translated three of Laforgue's sixteen "Locutions des Pierrots" ("Speeches," perhaps "Soliloquies," "of the Pierrots"; Laforgue sometimes spoke of Pierrots in the plural, as though they constituted a specific class, like the American Beatniks). A few months after that, when Crane came to write "Chaplinesque," he produced a remarkable fusion of images: his own image of the poet as tenderly comic and his own portrait of Chaplin; the Charlot of French commentary and the Pierrot of Laforgue; a portion of Whitman's comic hero; and something far older than any of these. The result is a figure of profoundly representative significance.

[5] Matthew Josephson in particular reported to Crane from Paris about the French fascination with the American cinema, which meant, as Josephson said, the films of Chaplin. The letter he quotes, however, as possibly stimulating "Chaplinesque" is dated some months after the poem was written. Josephson, *Life Among the Surrealists* (New York, 1962), pp. 123-26.

The immediate predecessors of Laforgue's Pierrot were two pantomimists of genius—Jean-Gaspard Deburau, who began to perform in a Parisian cellar known as *Theâtre des Funambules* in 1830, and Paul Legrand, who followed Deburau in the same little establishment in 1847. These two artists between them offered Jules Laforgue (and other poets, Gautier and Verlaine among them) a comic profile comparable in its poetic value to the one Chaplin supplied for Hart Crane. But what should be emphasized is the radical transformation effected by Deburau and Legrand upon the formerly conventional European clown. The conventional character was introduced into France by visiting Italian players in the early seventeenth century, and known variously in Italy and France through the centuries as Pagliaccio, Pedrolino, Arlecchino, Harlequin, Giles, Pierrot, and so forth. He was primarily a figure of robustious farce. He was usually a servant, and a boisterous and self-assertive one. He was also, so to speak, the butt of Eros; cuckolded himself, he was constantly duped in his clumsy efforts to cuckold others, though he was possessed of a vein of vulgar common sense to offset his customary blockheadedness. But Jean-Gaspard Deburau, a person of a melancholy and even suicidal temperament, invested that traditional bumpkin with his own quality of hard-earned, stoical self-control; Paul Legrand (in Enid Welsford's account) completed the metamorphosis of Pierrot by "introducing pathos and mystery into the character of the once rollicking clown."[6] By mid-century, Charles Baudelaire was noticing with sur-

[6] *The Fool* (New York, 1961), p. 310.

prise that the French Pierrot had become "pale as the moon, mysterious as silence, supple and mute as the serpent, long and lean as a pole" in contrast with the typical English clown who continued to be the old knockabout figure who "enters like a tempest, falls like a bale, and shakes the house when he laughs."[7] To adopt the phrases of Hart Crane, the everlasting eyes of Pierrot had, in France, quite replaced the laughter of Gargantua; and the dolorous figure with the painted smile had become a fact of French culture.

But in a sense Deburau and Legrand, and following them Laforgue, were reaching behind the Franco-Italian *clown*, who was mainly a Renaissance creation, to recover elements of the medieval *fool*—with a crucial difference, to be noted. The word "fool" is even more comprehensive and various than the word "clown"; it is a very complex word indeed, and its "structure," in William Empson's meaning, has a very complex and dialectical history.[8] For our limited purposes, however, we can apply the formula of Mr. Empson: since in the medieval view "all men are fools in the eyes of God," so the type of fool was exactly "Everyman in the presence of God." The human fool, so ridiculous and even contemptible to human eyes, was just the way any man, Everyman, looked when inspected by the Creator. As motleyed jester, as invented figure in poetry, drama, and impromptu festivals, the fool was a device for commenting on power, wealth, and intellect in an other-wordly perspective,

[7] *Ibid.*, p. 312.
[8] *The Structure of Complex Words* (Norfolk, Conn., 1952), p. 107.

one which allowed the comment to sound not only like precautionary good sense, but like humbling echoes of God's wisdom. He was, at the same time, a vehicle for acknowledging and celebrating those non-rational and antinomian aspects of human nature that a culture always suppresses or undervalues at its peril.

Some such concatenation of ideas seem to have turned up again, with a dialectical twist, in the nineteenth century, exemplified diversely by poets like Laforgue and Mallarmé, and by painters like Cézanne and the later Roualt, Picasso and Chagall. Those artists projected clown figures who are not eccentric and socially peripheral objects of mirth, but modes of the modern Everyman. Alluding to the painters just named, Wallace Fowlie has remarked that "as all women were in the painted Virgin of the Italian Renaissance, so all men are in the painted clown of modern France."[9] The clown so widely and modernly represented thus became once more the oldtime fool who commented on the established power of the day, upon a rationalistic, heartless, belligerent, scientific, and industrializing society. But only rarely can the modern fool be seen as Everyman in the presence of God. He is much rather Everyman confronting the absence of God, Everyman as he peers through a materialistic culture at an increasingly absurd universe in which he recognizes his own being—the human being itself—as irredeemably clownish. Examining this development, Father Martin D'Arcy has concluded somberly that the clown of modern painting and poetry bears "a pitiable resemblance to that of

[9] *The Clown's Grail* (London, 1947), pp. 114-15.

man crucified but without grace. The would-be hero (the image of God) is covered with grease paint, and exhibiting himself before a faceless audience in a play without meaning, without even the wisdom of the child, and certainly without its innocence."[10] A clown perhaps, but a dismal and a joyless one.

And finally, in the wake of the European Romantic movement, with its habit of filling out the picture of Man with the picture of the Creative Self, the modern clown is not only a transformed, melancholy image of Everyman in a senseless world, frequently he is also an image of the artist. In the world's view, he is a laughable entertainer; in his own view, he has a voice of sadness, even despair, muffled behind his clownish makeup. Such, anyhow, is one of the defining tendencies of *L'Art Pierrot* of Jules Laforgue.

The Pierrot whose "asides" we overhear in *L'Imitation de Notre Dame La Lune* is the earlier Deburau-Legrand figure unhappily beset by contradictions and especially troubled by the mysteries of sex. His is a condition helplessly divided against itself, mocking what it longs for, delicately despising what it has. "I am nothing but a lunar playboy," he confesses, "making circles in ponds." The moon for Laforgue was a sort of hollow unreality, a Romantic convention carefully emptied of meaning; in dedicating himself (in the volume's title-phrase) to an "imitation of Our Lady the moon," he is in fact deliberately accepting a career of nullity, even as he is carefully blaspheming aspects of the Christian tradition. Meanwhile, a natural fas-

[10] "The Clown and the Philosopher" in *The Month* (London), January, 1949, p. 8.

tidiousness of conduct is constantly betrayed by the erotic impulse, upon which in turn Laforgue's Pierrot takes his malicious and self-defeating revenge. He is still the butt of Eros; he complains about his lady's "perverse austerities," nurses a "divine infatuation" for Cydalise, and "fishes in troubled waters for Eve, Gioconda and Dalila" (the phrases quoted are in Hart Crane's translation). For recompense he reflects: "Yes, they are divine, those eyes! But nothing exists / Behind them! Her soul is a matter for the oculist." He scoffs at the notion of a woman "taking herself seriously in this century," and notices with exaggerated surprise that the lady has begun to weep.

At moments like this, Pierrot is Man in the sense of Male, caught up in the endless and debasing round of sexual cross-purposes, a fact which annoyed Jacques Rivière, who remarked that "that *idée fixe* of [Laforgue] is really exasperating. After all . . . there are so many other things." But as Warren Ramsay has pointed out, "if a poet happens to be a romantic, even a late-blooming and ironical one, the misunderstanding between the sexes may stand for other apprehensions, the one between the poet and society, for example."[11] Pierrot's amatory difficulties have an air of actuality, and one feels that if they could have been overcome, he might have been consoled for the parallel difficulties, the felt foolishness, of the artistic effort. But they are also no doubt a bitter-comic representation of Pierrot's relation—that is, the relation of the artist in Laforgue's generation—to the "perverse aus-

[11] *Jules Laforgue and the Ironic Inheritance* (New York, 1953), p. 189. I am especially beholden to Mr. Ramsay's chapter on Laforgue and Hart Crane.

terities" of the modern world, a world he at once courts and denigrates, a world which may claim to love him but has not the wit to understand a word he says. Both the dim-sighted world and an imagined lady are present in the artist-lover's report: "She whispered: 'I am waiting, here I am, I don't know ...' Her gaze having taken on broad lunar ingenuousness."[12] The skeptical and hesitant Laforguian figure is less mysterious and pathetic than the clown of Deburau and Legrand, but it reveals a vein of wistfulness that cynicism never quite excises. His frustrated love affair with the world could provide a paradigm for Hart Crane's more touching, more joyful, and more fertilely moon-struck image of the clown-poet who can still love the world, thwarted as he may be by its heavy-handed hostility.

The paradigm, however, came to Crane at first through the mediation of T. S. Eliot and (less so) of Ezra Pound. As an undergraduate at Harvard, Eliot had discovered Laforgue in Arthur Symons' book, *The Symbolist Movement in French Literature,* and had written a number of poems that he himself located *"sous la ligne de Laforgue."* Eliot was for some years intrigued to the point of obsession (as he much later acknowledged) by a number of elements in Laforgue's

[12] Translation by Henri Peyre in *The Poem Itself* (Cleveland, 1962). Part of Professor Peyre's commentary can be quoted as a very apt summary of the whole development I have been discussing: "The poet (the artist in Mallarmé and Picasso) sees himself as a clown whose profession it is to entertain, but whose white-faced mask expresses longing for the one consolation against the senselessness of the world: feminine tenderness. . . . But the feminine declaration of love for him alone and forever . . . arouses his most waggish banter" (p. 63).

work, including Laforgue's ironical manipulation of older legends and stories like those of Parsifal and Hamlet;[13] he was, however, perhaps especially drawn to the Pierrot poems, to their verbal and rhythmical innovations, and to the rueful imagery he could find in them, imagery which represented the modern sensibility hesitating and bemused among the perplexities, erotic and otherwise, of modern life. Something of this hovers in such Laforguian poems of Eliot as "Conversation Galante," "Portrait of a Lady," and "La Figlia che Piange"; it reaches full statement in "The Love Song of J. Alfred Prufrock," "the great example of the Laforguian poem in English," according to Malcolm Cowley.[14] Here the lover's wistfulness is less contaminated by self-defense and his gesture even more ineffectual than in Laforgue; Prufrock accepts his role not as Prince Hamlet, but as a Polonius who is only a step away from being the court's comic relief—

> Full of high sentence, but a bit obtuse;
> At times, indeed, almost ridiculous—
> Almost, at times, the Fool.

This is obviously a portrait of the artist as well as the confession of a lover; if the capitalized word "Fool" suggests momentarily some paradoxical superiority in

[13] See Leonard Unger's long essay, "Laforgue, Conrad and T. S. Eliot," in *The Man in the Name* (Minneapolis, Minn., 1956).

[14] "Laforgue in America: A Testimony"; *Sewanee Review*, Winter, 1963. Mr. Cowley lists the following characteristics as peculiarly Laforguian: "the urban background, the timidly yearning hero . . . the self-protective irony, the bold figures of speech, the mixture of colloquial and academic language, the rhythms that might be those of popular song, and the rhyming couplets serving as refrains." Most, though not all, of those characteristics can be detected in Crane's "Chaplinesque."

either role—as in the medieval Fool of Love—it is not, I think, a hint that long survives.

Eliot introduced Ezra Pound to Laforgue around 1914. It was the expressed enthusiasm of the two writers for the French poet that drew so many youthful American *literati* to Laforgue after the war when, as Malcolm Cowley has recalled, "the complete works of Jules Laforgue gathered dust" on almost every mantelpiece in Greenwich Village. Back in Cleveland, in 1920, Hart Crane was moved to send to Paris for several volumes of Laforgue, and he felt at once, as he wrote Allen Tate, "a certain sympathy with Laforgue's attitude," his attitude, presumably, towards the follies and dilemmas of the poet and the lover in modern times. In any case, Crane's sympathy was sufficient for him to translate three of the sixteen *Locutions des Pierrots*.

Each of the three is a combination of complaint, taunt, and plea addressed to or concerning some young lady: some *"vaillante oisive femme"* in Laforgue's phrase; in Crane's, some "prodigal and wholly dilatory lady." When Crane's versions were published in the *Double Dealer* in 1922, he added a note saying "A strictly literal translation of Laforgue is meaningless. The native implications of his idiosyncratic style have to be recast in English garments." He remarked defensively to Allen Tate that "no one ought to be particularly happy about a successful translation," and that he only did these "for fun." In fact, Crane's "Locutions" are less translations than (to borrow the Nietzschean word of which Crane would have approved) they are transvaluations of the original; as

such, they have an unexpected interest. For one thing,
Crane sometimes used the line structure of Laforgue's
verse simply as a frame within which to practice his
own brand of language: *"la lune-levante de ma belle
âme"* (literally, "the moonrise of my handsome soul")
thus provides the occasion for Crane's "the orient
moon of my dapper affections." But more important, as even that single example suggests, what
Crane was really doing was to diminish, very nearly
to expunge, the irony that everywhere permeated
Laforgue's poetry and his vision. To focus on the key
symbol, Crane restores substance and value to the dis-
empowered moon.

The process can be best illustrated via the third of
the "Locutions." In Laforgue, this begins:

> *Ah! sans lune, quelles nuits blanches,*
> *Quel cauchemars pleins de talent!*
> *Vois-je pas là nos cygnes blancs,*
> *Vient-on pas de tourner la clenche?*
>
> *Et c'est vers toi que j'en suis là.*
> *Que ma conscience voit double,*
> *Et que mon coeur pêche en eau troublé*
> *Eve, Joconde et Dalila!*

Crane renders the lines as follows:

> Ah! without the moon, what white nights,
> What nightmares rich with ingenuity!
> Don't I see your white swans there?
> Doesn't someone come to turn the knob?
>
> And it's your fault that I'm this way,
> That my conscience sees double,
> And my heart fishes in troubled waters
> For Eve, Gioconda and Dalila.

An almost fundamental change is effected at the out-

set when, "without the moon," Crane experiences
"nightmares rich with ingenuity" against Laforgue's
"*cauchemars pleins de talents.*" Instead of Laforgue's
polished irony, which quietly drains the force out
every allusion, Crane offers a direct, if packed, statement about the creative imagination. For Crane, unlike Laforgue, still believed in the moon, and in the
power it symbolized, the power, as he would say in
"Chaplinesque," to make "a grail of laughter of an
empty ash can." So believing, he could feel the strug-
gling nightmare of the moon's absence, the ingenuities
contrived to overcome its loss. Beneath Laforgue's
surface there is also of course considerable seriousness
and some anguish, but by and large, he seems to play
—very skilfully—with the adversities of poet and
lover, while Crane gives back to them their exigent
reality. And by so contending with, by measuring
himself against, the most ironical of modern European poets (all in the guise of translation), Crane's
emotional honesty as well as the peculiarities of his
genius forced him to take a first step away from irony
itself, or beyond it. For a writer of his temperament,
no step could have been more necessary at the time.

This is not to say that in his "Locutions" Crane
pursued a uniform course, or that he was uniformly
successful. He failed, on the whole, in the matter of
rhythm. Laforgue's rhythms were themselves devices
of irony, and in them his ironic attitudes found their
perfect tone, almost a monotone;[15] but "confronted by

[15] Though perhaps less so than one might suppose. Malcolm
Cowley, in the article cited, has pointed out what few of the
early American Laforguians realized: the dependence of Laforgue
upon popular songs and children's chants.

the relaxed rhythms of Laforgue," as Warren Ramsay has observed, "Crane is technically ill at ease." He was at least ill at ease when he attempted to simulate the original rhythm, rather than to transform it. One plainly hears Crane's natural impulse towards a stronger, more exclamatory and dramatic statement being hampered by a line like: "And it's your fault that I'm this way"; whereas in the original (*"Et c'est vers toi que je suis là"*), the sounds fall into place smoothly enough. The restraining influence of Laforgue can also be heard in Crane's poem "My Grandmother's Love Letters"; it produced a rather debilitating effect in "The Bridge at Estador": "I do not know what you'll see,—your vision/ May slumber yet in the moon." Even there the Laforguian elements—tone, image, cadence—were of undeniable value to Crane as he groped after his own idiom and music. Crane's involvement with Laforgue was a significant chapter in his career; to have maintained it, however, would have proved fatal.

But of this there had in fact been little chance. Throughout his Laforguian phase, Crane had been a good deal more vulnerable than, say, Eliot had been to diametrically opposite poetic persuasions, including a diametrically opposite comic image. Eliot could beautifully absorb and be absorbed by Laforgue because the latter's witty self-deprecation could add salt to Eliot's incipient and, as it would develop, profound strain of Christian humility. But while Hart Crane was congenitally modest, and although he too took on for a while the mask of self-derision, there was in him no great tendency toward Christian humility—not, in any case, toward that dark Jansenistic kind that Eliot stood for. Unlike Eliot, Crane was always responsive to the poetry of braggadocio. In his view, the doleful eyes of Pierrot were intended not to replace, but to blend with the laughter of Gargantua. In somewhat simplistic literary terms, the spirit of Jules Laforgue mingled in Crane's imagination with a spirit at once more robust and more American, to which we can give the name of Walt Whitman.

He was aided in this regard by his own ignorance. Certain educated friends, Crane wrote Tate in 1922, had lamented the fact that he (Crane) had been taken to Laforgue "without having placed [him] in relation to most of the older 'classics,' which I haven't read. . . . Nonetheless, my affection for Laforgue is none the less genuine for being led to him through Pound and Eliot than it would have been through Baudelaire." Inevitably, he missed some of the implications of Laforgue's references—the accretions his moon, his swans, his ladies brought with them from earlier French poetry. But for the same reason, Laforgue was a more easily displaceable burden for Crane than for Eliot; two years after the letter just quoted, Crane would allude deprecatingly to "the consciously-contrived 'Pierrots' of Laforgue," and two years after that, more harshly yet, he would describe Laforgue's general attitude as a sort of fastidious whimper. There are, to be sure, clear echoes of Laforgue as late as *The Bridge*, especially in the sad, erotic play of "Three Songs," when Laforgue's image of the poet "fishing in troubled waters/ For Eve, Gioconda and Dalila" can be heard (transvaluated, as always) in the sound of names falling "vainly on the waves/ Eve! Magdalene!/ Or Mary, you?" Meanwhile, there had been all along another powerful element at work in Crane. If he knew rather less than his educated friends about the French literary tradition, he knew or perhaps guessed rather more about the American. "Chaplinesque" participates in a specifically American comic tradition. It is one that takes its principal start with Whitman, a tradition that, given fresh impetus by Hart Crane, has progressed to the point where it is prabably the most vital aspect of American writing at the present day. Crane's place in this development illustrates as well as anything could his great talent for projecting images not only forceful but roundly representative: a talent that makes him, on balance, the most immediately communicative of twentieth-century American poets.

## III

The poet-hero who announced his appearance amid the eccentric typography of the Preface to the 1855 *Leaves of Grass* was a comic figure of an already thoroughly familiar sort. He was, in fact, a vast verbal enlargement of the *persona* known for more than half a century as the Yankee. The latter, like the clown of the older European comedy troupes, was by convention a comic servant; and, as Daniel Hoffman has remarked, he "first walks on the stage as the rustic Jonathan in Royall Tyler's famous comedy, *The Contrast*,"[16] a play (1797) in the sub-plot of which the native American type is given a provisional profile by

---

[16] *Form and Fable in American Fiction* (New York, 1961), p. 46.

"contrast" between his honest if slow-witted sturdiness and the simpering affectations of another servant named Jessamy. It was by just such contrasts with the Europeanized personality that the first recognizable new-world character got itself defined; if, in the comparison, the American looked oafish and ignorant, he also seemed stalwart, morally pure, and sometime surprisingly shrewd. The shrewdness and the purity eventually separated, and (Mr. Hoffman has traced this for us) the confidence man and the uncouth crusader would pursue separate or embattled careers through decade after decade. On the whole, however, we may take as *the* Yankee that virtuous dolt who stumbled untainted through villanies and temptations from the late eighteenth century on.[17] It was this figure that Whitman brought to full scale, and upon which he worked certain key and magical transformations.

Whitman, indeed, had an even more pronounced effect upon the American comic hero and the tradition in which that hero flourished than Laforgue did in France; it is worth remembering that just as Hart Crane had been reading and translating Laforgue's Pierrot poems prior to writing "Chaplinesque," so Laforgue had been reading and translating Whitman prior to *L'Imitation de Notre Dame La Lune*. Laforgue was perhaps more interested in Whitman's metrics than in his substance, but the two aspects cannot at all be divided; for Whitman, no less than for Laforgue, rhythms were an essential part of the comic

[17] In fiction such a character can be followed from, say, Brockden Brown's *Arthur Mervyn* (1797) up to and beyond Thornton Wilder's classic version, *Heaven's My Destination* (1936).

posture and utterance. The clownish figure in Whitman's poetry is, in fact, less a persistent human character than a hovering presence, and a presence felt above
all in the play of language and twist of meter. The
human character comes through clearly enough in the
1855 *Preface:* boastful, naive, adventurous, a bit uncouth, and a brash lover of all creation: the Yankee
as comical culture hero. In the earlier European manner, he "enters like a tempest"; and in the American
manner, he is identified in all his differences from
poets of other countries. The animating motif in the
1855 poems is at many moments antic and bizarre,
the figure we watch and listen to is given to sudden
fits of clowning; a nose-thumbing irreverence and an
impish desire to shock alternate with Whitman's peculiar erotic religiosity and his moods of rapture and
awe. Even so death-haunted a poem as "The Sleepers"
is interrupted by a shriek of comic horror ("O for
pity's sake, no one must see me now! . . . my clothes
were stolen while I was abed"). Still, the comedy is
even more centrally a matter of technique.

It is Whitman's language that performs the function of clown, and no one put the case more precisely
than Whitman himself. "Considering language, then,
as some mighty potentate," he wrote in an early prose
passage, "into the majestic audience-hall of the mon-
arch ever enters a personage like one of Shakespeare's
clowns, and takes possession there and plays a part
even in the stateliest ceremonies. Such is Slang, or
indirection. . . ." Most of Whitman's long debated
verbal inventions belongs to his comic purpose; his
statement to Traubel in the late days at Camden that

"I sometimes think the *Leaves* is only a language experiment" is almost exactly parallel to his statement during the same period that "I pride myself on being a real humorist underneath everything else."[18] Nor was the allusion to Shakespeare's clowns merely vague, or grandiose, for Whitman's comedy of language proceeded in a manner very close to Shakespeare's comedy of action. In Shakespeare, the comic dimension provides an indispensable corrective by parodying the serious or tragic element so as to cast the latter in an ambiguous—hence a truer—light. In Whitman it is not simply the slang, it is the audible slang in the midst of "the stateliest ceremonies" of speech that provides the comedy. We hear not only "blab" and "chuff" and "drib" and "hap" and "lag" and "swash" and "yawp," we hear those blunt verbal bullets as they ricochet off the stately and pretentious sides of words like "presidentiad" and "cartouche" and "ambulanza" and "imperturbe" and "lumine" and "sonnambula." If we add to this the coiling unconventionality of Whitman's rhythm, with its capacity to leap or to relax, to startle or assuage at will, we are close to the heart of Whitman's comedy— or perhaps to any authentic comic verse.

But there is another exceedingly significant aspect to Whitman's comedy, one that comes into prominence in the late 1850s. In the poems of 1855 and 1856, both human nature and the creative enterprise were subjected to a sort of cheerful curative mockery only occasionally darkened by real doubt. In the 1860

---

[18] Richard Chase, in *Walt Whitman Revisited* (New York, 1955), has given the best account of Whitman as a comic poet.

edition, a new note appeared: new, that is, in Whitman and in American poetry, but remarkably similar to the note struck earlier in France. Whitman's comic sensibility, while not less prevalent than before, had deepened into a mysterious and melancholy sense of his own moral and artistic inadequacy. Some of the 1860 poems reflect a dolorousness like that of the French pantomimist, some a half-buried suicidal impulse like that of Jean-Gaspard Deburau, and some a sense of creative frustration which anticipates Laforgue. Pierrot joined Gargantua in these poems, and the junction is nowhere more impressive than in "As I Ebb'd with the Ocean of Life." Here, in a poem largely about psychic and artistic annihilation, Whitman introduced a supreme example of the poet's self-derision: an image of the poet and all his works mocked by what Whitman called the Real Me:

> Withdrawn far, mocking me with mock-
>     congratulatory signs and bows,
> With peals of distant ironical laughter at every
>     word I have written,
> Pointing in silence to these songs, and then
>     to the sand beneath.

The Real Me was Whitman's "Oversoul," his divine muse. In the lines quoted, we have Whitman's version of the poet as fool, the poet as Everyman in the presence of his special God; of the way the most ambitious of human efforts looks in the mocking perspective of divinity.

Hart Crane presumably came to Whitman, as all too many readers have come to him, from the wrong end: via those prophetic or patriotic or "cosmic" chants behind which the best of Whitman lay hidden till recently, and on the basis of which Whitman earned a quite unjustified reputation for humorlessness. It is the cosmic Whitman whose hand Crane would clasp in the "Cape Hatteras" section of *The Bridge*. But Crane was always a tough-minded judge of poetry, and no less of Whitman's poetry. "You've heard me roar at too many of his lines," he reminded Tate in 1930, "to doubt that I can spot his worst, I'm sure." Something of Whitman's best—his verbal sporting, for example, and his sense of the irresistible flow of experience—is reflected elsewhere in *The Bridge*. Crane's imaginative association with Whitman appears to have grown abruptly with the first conception of *The Bridge* in 1923. But it also appears that at some earlier stage Crane was infected, in the secretive manner of poetic influence, by Whitman's conception of the poet as something between a comedian and a divinity (a conception that was especially pervasive in Whitman's writing before the Civil War). Even in "Chaplinesque" there is a sort of implicit capering, almost a bumptiousness, a quality that for lack of a better adjective and to distinguish it from the Gallic irony that it pushes against, we can only call American; which, for Crane at this time, is the same as to call it Whitmanian.

The matter is interestingly beclouded by Whitman's diversity, including the diversity of his comic spirit. The force of Whitman's example is equally felt in another account of the poet as clown, one much longer and more intricate than "Chaplinesque" and completed a year after Crane's poem: "The Comedian as the Letter C," by the most cultivated of Whitman's literary grand-nephews, Wallace Stevens. But here the example works to a different effect. At one moment in this lengthy mock-epic, its wandering undersized hero, Crispin, is observed stopping "in the dooryard of his own capacious bloom." That echo of Whitman's most famous poem nearly defines the comic essence of Stevens's work, for it is as though Stevens were openly setting his own frustrated efforts beside Whitman's great achievement, as though Whitman himself were Stevens's Real Me, and a power audible in the background who mocks Stevens "with distant ironical laughter at every word" Stevens had written. The poetic effort whose failure is comically narrated is an effort to do what Whitman had done: to render in poetry the hard, resistant, and multiple reality of America. The surface of Stevens's poem is preternaturally alive with verbal comedy of a recognizably Whitmanian kind: an extraordinary interplay of the stately, the colloquial, the boldly invented, the bizarre, the imported. But the story told in that dazzling language belongs to comedy of a different but equally familiar order, the comedy of ruefully admitted defeat, the mask of witty self-deprecation.

"The Comedian as the letter C" is, among other things, an ironic autobiography, the poet's unsparing history of his own consciousness and how it got that way: a satiric version, so to speak, of "Song of Myself." It is the story of a poet who began, as many American poets did begin around 1900 (when Stevens, born 1879, reached his majority) by writing "his couplet yearly to the spring," by writing "poems of plums," by affecting an air of "decorous melancholy" and the pseudo-exotic ("cloak of China, cap of Spain, imperative haw of hum"). One thinks of those triple-named versifiers (like Edward Clarence Stedman) who ruled the poetic fashion at the turn of the century. "Maya sonneteers," Stevens calls them: poets who despite the splendid native birds available and "still to the night-bird" (nightingale) "made their plea, / As if rasberry tanagers in palms, / High up in orange air, were barbarous." Stevens's young hero commits himself to the native and the barbarous to escape from the "stale intelligence" of "his fellows," and to scrawl "With his own quill, in its indigenous dew." And it is here that Stevens refers to him as "a clown perhaps, but an aspiring clown."

The aspiration to abandon the stale or irrelevant European tradition, and to face up poetically to twentieth-century America is not ignoble. It takes the structural form of a voyage from the coast of France to eastern America: "Bordeaux to Yucatan, Havana next, / And then to Carolina. Simple jaunt." The journey from the old world to the new is shaped in epic style. It is cast deliberately in the mould of the classical literary epic: the departure from the old world, the difficult and dangerous sea-crossing, the tentative landings and fresh adventures, the arrival at the site of the new home, the effort to found a new society and a new culture. But the aspiration is also clownish, and the outward structure mocks the inner journey, which is a journey of poetic awareness and attitude, an attempt to cross over from the genteel to the vulgarly alive, from the artificial to the real, and from one aspect of the self to another. In "The Comedian" that effort fails, as it had historically failed with certain other poets, if not in fact with Wallace Stevens. Those "young Harvard poets," as George Santayana would say retrospectively, "hadn't enough stamina to stand up to their country and describe it as a poet should . . . Being educated men, they couldn't pitch their voices or find their inspiration in that strident society."[19] Thus for the hapless Crispin, despite his good intentions:

> America was always north to him,
> A northern west or western north, but north,
> And thereby polar, polar-purple, chilled
> And lank, rising and slumping from a sea
> Of hardy foam, receding flatly, spread
> In endless ledges, glittering, submerged
> And cold in a boreal mistiness of the moon. . . .
> It was a flourishing tropic he required.

Confronted by that northern, chilled, lank, slumping, flat, misty landscape, Crispin's tropical spirit is defeated. He yields to mere domestication, and after beginning on his adventure "with a green brag," he concludes "fadedly . . . as a man prone to distemper," "Fickle and fumbling, variable, obscure, Glozing his life with after-shining flicks."

If Stevens did not personally conclude with such fading and fumbling, it was because he adopted the strategy that Santayana (in the letter quoted) wisely

[19] Letter to V. F. Calverton, November 18, 1934; quoted from the Calverton papers (New York Public Library) by Daniel Aaron, in his introduction to Robert Herrick's *Memoirs of a Citizen* (Cambridge, Mass., 1962), p. vi.

observed as the only strategy capable of handling the
stridencies of America in verse—that of satire. More
cunningly still, Stevens not only treated the native actualities satirically, he satirised the poetic effort to treat
them at all. He mocked both the discordant world and
the poet in relation to it. He assumed for a time the only
role that made survival possible, the role of the poet
as comedian; and only after having done so could he
go on, some years later, to the complex serenities of
his extraordinary middle-age and old-age writing. In
"The Comedian" even Santayana's reference to the
poets' trying to pitch their voices amid the American
noise is ironically anticipated in Crispin's decision to
find "a new reality in parrot-squawks." But the central symbol is the poem's hero himself.

Crispin is as fruitful a choice for Stevens as Pierrot
had been for Laforgue and Charlie Chaplin for Hart
Crane; or for that matter, the Yankee had been for
Whitman. Like Pierrot, Crispin belonged originally
to the Italo-French comic traditions, especially to the
Commedia del Arte; and like both Pierrot and the
American Yankee, he was initially a comical servant.
But Crispin's clowning had never consisted in enter-
ing like a tempest and falling like a bale. He had been
a far more canny and urbane person; his comic pattern had been to hurry back and forth, with a sort of
adroit desperation, between two different and incompatible masters, trying without their knowledge to
serve as valet to both at once. The Crispin of Wallace
Stevens is the French valet transplanted and made into
a clownish American poet, just as in the poem's "plot,"
Crispin leaves the French port and winds up some-

where on the North American continent. But the new
Crispin gets caught in the same old predicament. He
must once again try to serve two masters, or to do
justice to two very different dimensions. The latter
are given a variety of names in the poem: Europe and
America, north and south, and so on, but they are
primarily the two poles of Stevens's continuing dia-
lectic. They are the imagination and the real, and their
chief symbols here are those familiar Romantic ones,
the moon and the sun. Even as he arrives in North
America and inspects its "Arctic moonlight," Crispin,
longing for the sun, realizes that his poetic and spiritual voyaging must always be "An up and down between two elements, / A fluctuating between sun and
moon." The lines are a summary account of almost
the whole body of Stevens's poetry. But here, in "The
Comedian as the Letter C," the venture is made to
seem merely hazardous and ridiculous; and Crispin in
that poem appears as the Buster Keaton of poets.

Mention of that splendid silent film comedian can
remind us again—as "Chaplinesque" reminds us—that
the comic image in literature during Hart Crane's
generation could draw much from its counterpart on
film. Along with the evasive buffoonery of Chaplin,
there were such brilliant figures as Buster Keaton and
Harry Langdon, who also knew how to intermix the
mirthful with the pathetic, a fragment of Gargantua
with a portion of Pierrot; after them came Harpo
Marx, whose comic genius rivalled Chaplin's, and
who, like Crane's Chaplin, managed to skip by the
hefty obstructions of officialdom and still love the
world. These were only at several removes images of

the artist. They were chiefly images of modern man sprung loose in an utterly random and yet mysteriously hostile universe, a universe in which persons, and more importantly somehow, *things* conspired against the individual whose "only ally" (as Frank Capra once said about Langdon) "was God."[20] The silent comedians (their achievement greatly aided by silence) comprised a sizeable and enduring element in the history of modern culture; they are easily recognizable as the predecessors of the hurrying hero in American fiction since the second war; they have been acknowledged as contributing significantly to the European "theater of the absurd." But within the narrower confines of literature itself, it was e. e. cummings, after Crane and Stevens, who did most to advance the comic view of both man and artist, to suggest indeed, as he did in a play of 1928 called *him*, that it was because he was a man, that the artist was a comedian.

In *him*, the dominant metaphor becomes strict, and the contemporary American artist is presented almost literally as a circus clown, a member of the Ringling Brothers troupe. *Him* is a wonderfully bewildering combination of farce, surrealism, sex and its various perversions, poignancy, dream (both old-fashioned and Freudian), political and cultural satire, and tough stuff. It borrows something from Pirandello's exploitation of the very notion of theatrical make-believe, and it looks forward, especially in the grave vacuities of the three choral Miss Weirds—the Misses Stop, Look, and Listen—to the early plays of Ionesco. The play's

[20] *Agee on Film* (New York, 1958), p. 14.

subject, as the hero "him" explains about his own play to the heroine "me," is "the sort of man—who is writing a play about a man who is writing a sort of play"; a satirical tail-piece to Romantic narcissism. But the focus throughout is on the nature of the artist, and here, a year before Charlie Chaplin's film *The Circus*, the artist shows up as a clownish acrobat.

In a number of lyric poems, then and later, cummings radiated a comic spirit alternately robust and wistful, coarse and tender, Rabelaisian and Pierrotesque, a series of surrogates for the aggressive or sensitive imagination. His proud dream-horse, moving smooth-loomingly through the cluttered city streets, is one such; so is the little lame balloon-man; so, in the more vigorous mode, is cummings' Buffalo Bill, that handsome man, "who used to break onetwothreefourfive pigeonsjustlikethat!" In *him*, the definition includes some of Buffalo Bill's daring, but the rodeo is replaced by the circus, the clowning is more emphatic, and the accomplishment less assured. Reading the hero's palm, the second Miss Weird (Miss Look) tells him accurately: "Your favorite planet is Ringling Brothers"; and "him" rephrases Wordsworth to declaim oracularly, "Barnum thou shouldst be living at this hour."

"Damn everything but the circus," he cries impatiently. He means: damn every account of life, modern life, except the one that sees it as a circus; that is why the world needs Barnum at this hour. On the original dust jacket, cummings said in a note that his play was intended to represent the realm where doing and dreaming interact: not the meaning of life, but its being, the thing itself. Toward this aim the play in its final act dissolves "reality" altogether into a circus, complete with freaks and sideshows and fortune-tellers and barkers. It is within this perspective on modern experience and behavior that the artist is identified. "The average 'painter' 'sculptor' 'poet' 'composer' 'playwright'," says "him" to "me" contemptuously, "is a person who cannot leap through a hoop from a galloping horse, make people laugh with the clown's mouth, orchestrate twenty lions." But the true and superior artist can do just those things, or has to attempt them; he must try—given the frenetic expectancies of the modern audience—to be simultaneously daredevil, clown, and lion-tamer. "Him" is more recklessly ambitious yet. "Imagine," he continues, "a human being who balances three chairs, one on top of the other, on a wire, eight feet in the air with no net underneath and then climbs into the top chair, sits down and begins to swing. . . . I am that." Carried away by his image, "him" continues into pure fantasy: he imagines that three chairs are kicked away, and that the artist resides thereafter on top of three impalpable "facts." He does not stay there long. The very formula of his profession requires that he shortly plunge into the sawdust, to the infinite excitement and delight of his audience. For his three facts are the facts that he is an artist; and yet he is a man; and so, his unlimited aspiration mocked by his humanity, he is a failure.

## IV

The confession is made without bitterness. There is in it, instead, a surprising amount of pure joy, along

with an accent of gaiety. In his *Six Nonlectures* of
1953, cummings provided his own gloss on the "three
facts" of *him* in a characteristic spray of polysyllables,
contending that " 'an artist, a man, a failure' is no
mere whenfully accreting mechanism, but a givingly
eternal complexity—neither some soulless and heartless ultrapredatory infra-animal nor any un-under-
standingly knowing and believing and thinking au-
tomaton, but a naturally and miraculously whole
human being—a feelingly illimitable individual, whose
only happiness is to transcend himself, whose every
agony is to grow." That "feelingly illimitable individual," whose actual limitations are countered and
overcome by a passionate urge towards self-transcen-
dence, resembles the person celebrated by cummings
in "My Father Moved Through Dooms of Love."
But he will hardly appear to resemble some of the
other figures in the comic tradition I have been examining: the deeply melancholy Deburau; the Pierrot,
at once self-deriding and malicious, of Laforgue; the
ebbing Whitman of 1860, mocked from afar; the
minuscule Crispin, his bravado all faded, of Stevens.
One might well conclude that the really significant
development in the comic mode, both at home and
abroad, over the past century or so has been the de-
ployment of comedy as a way of registering artistic
and human defeat, and the use of the clown figure as
a means of living with despair. And yet a note of
something more than sheer endurance ("I laugh that
I may not weep"), a note implying an unexpected
victory of sorts—victory over all the forces that try
to make life and art impossible—a note even of posi-

tive joy, these too are inherent in the comic tradition, and are part of the clownish profile. They are audible, of course, in the last lines of "Chaplinesque," and in a way that can be illuminated retroactively by looking for a moment at one or two much later compositions.

Nathaniel West, for example, contributed unforgettably to the modern image of the tortured clown in *Miss Lonelyhearts* of 1933, but in *The Day of the Locust* (1939), he suggested less appalling, more beguiling, and perhaps more mature aspects of the clown figure. In *Miss Lonelyhearts*, the title figure, a hopelessly aspiring and helplessly absurd newspaper columnist, advances upon the world in a very fever of salvation, only to be shot dead on the spot. West's sick-souled missionary is the Savior as clown; amid the cynical and violent and dehumanized actualities of the time, his impulse of charity, his radically Christian ambitions, seem suicidally ridiculous. *The Day of the Locust*, however, or rather one key phase of it, is more reminiscent of the end of "Chaplinesque." West's last novel is charged with apocalyptic vision, but he introduced a minor yet vivid character named Harry Greener, who carries a small, significant hint about a condition beyond apocalypse. Greener is a one-time vaudeville comic whose stage personality had once been defined (in a newspaper) as that of "a bedraggled Harlequin." Greener's act as described is an unmistakeable microcosm of the recurring *action* in a good many recent American novels, those by Ralph Ellison, Bernard Malamud, James Purdy, Flannery O'Connor, J. D. Salinger, and others; here as in so many other ways, West (who died in 1941) is the first and perhaps the chief of the "post-war novelists." The act is an antic symbol of the individual's effort to make contact with the world, and the nature of the world's response. Greener comes on stage, full of anxious smiles and hopeful gestures, seeking recognition by a family of acrobats (the Ling family, "four musical Orientals"). He makes a shuffling plea that his own innocent affection be reciprocated, and the effort is met by a kick in the belly and a savage blow on the neck while the audience begins to laugh approvingly at the crippling pain he must endure. But endure he does, and at the end "he is tattered and bloody, but still sweet. . . . His is the final victory; the applause is for him." In context, the passage is beset by irony; and yet the suggestion has been made of an odd victory, oddly arrived at through a sort of comic humility and the instinct of love.

Closer yet to the content and spirit of "Chaplinesque" is one of Henry Miller's more engaging works, a long short story of 1948 called *The Smile at the Foot of the Ladder.* Up to a point, this is a spelling-out of Crane's poem (though Miller does not mention it). The story was written, Miller explains, for Fernand Leger, "to accompany a series of forty illustrations on clowns and circuses." The American edition carries reproductions of clown paintings and lithographs by Klee, Picasso, Chagall, Roualt, Toulouse-Lautrec, and de Segonzac;[21] Miller quite evidently wanted his little fable to catch at the mysterious essence of the clown's widespread appeal in the modern age. The narrative

[21] A Merle Armitage book, printed by the *Progress-Bulletin* for Duell, Sloan and Pearce (New York, 1948).

encompasses the short, happy life of the clown Auguste, whose circus act consisted entirely of sitting
"at the foot of a ladder reaching to the moon" (a
moon nailed to the roof of the tent), with "the lustre
of [an] extraordinary smile" engraved on his "sad
countenance." This trance-like meditation unaccount-
ably arouses his audience, night after night, to roars
of laughter and wild applause. But Auguste is dis-
contented; he wants not to make people laugh, but
"to endow his spectators with a joy which would
prove imperishable" by making them privy to the
vision he himself has had of a world beyond this tangible world, the world of the moon—a place of absolute beauty and unlimited joy. He quits the circus
and wanders abroad, passing through several adventures until he becomes innocently responsible for the
death of another and less aspiring clown, Antoine.
Auguste abandons all concealing garb and borrowed
personalities, and determines to be entirely his own
individual self. It is *as* himself that, seated one day on
a park bench, he has a mystical experience of the
absolute world; he moves towards it, and encounters
only "a man in uniform, armed with a club," who
strikes him down and kills him. Bystanders who hurry
to the side of the policeman's victim are astonished to
see that the dead Auguste is "smiling. . . . The eyes
were open, gazing with a candor unbelievable at the
thin sliver of a moon which had just become visible
in the heavens."

Miller's Auguste, like West's newspaperman, thus
suffers the doom that Hart Crane's Chaplin (at least
for the duration of the poem) manages to "dally";

with Auguste, the world's inevitable policeman has his brutal way. Miller, however, saw in his tale an allegory of Christian proportions. "A clown is a poet in action," he wrote. "He *is* the story which he enacts. It is the same story over and over—adoration, devotion, crucifixion." But crucifixion, like the crucifixion of Christ, can make the world reborn; and Miller saw Auguste's death "not as an end but as a beginning. When Auguste becomes himself life begins —and not just for Auguste but for all mankind." The spirit of candor, innocence, and joy, when fully realized in the individual self can, so Miller's implication rather hazily runs, save the world, however much it be cuffed about or beaten down. Crane in "Chaplinesque" suggests something less than this, and also something more.

On a personal level, Crane adopted the mask of comedy in his poem to the same end that Stevens did in "The Comedian as the Letter C": simply as a device for poetic survival in a society that despised art or a world (an America) not susceptible to it. But the comic role reaped unexpectedly large rewards for Crane, both in his career and within the poem. It was just because he accepted the role of comedian that the joint figure in "Chaplinesque" arrives at a sort of sacred vision:

> The game enforces smirks. But we have seen
> The moon in lonely alleys make
> A grail of laughter of an empty ash-can.

Crane's major development is here in small: from the enforced smirk to the grail of laughter; from the comic spirit to the religious spirit; from clownish consent to overwhelming visionary affirmation. "Chaplinesque" is in this sense the touchstone of Crane's early career; there is an organic continuity between it and the poem he began to write four months after its publication, "For the Marriage of Faustus and Helen," a poem in which the irony still present in "Chaplinesque" becomes altogether transcended. At the same time, on a level higher and broader than the personal, "Chaplinesque" contains insinuations (one dare not use a stronger word) vaster even than those claimed for his fable by Henry Miller.

They are insinuations about an epochal overturn in cultural and spiritual history, and their flickering presence in "Chaplinesque" is due to Crane's skill, compounded of literary awareness, spontaneous intuition, and sheer luck, in fusing several different and even contradictory comic traditions. The nineteenth-century French clown, mournful and agile, is reanimated in "Chaplinesque" through the immediate influence of Laforgue and Eliot, but he is reanimated in tonalities that at the same time recover a good deal of the medieval fool of which the French Pierrot had been a scrupulously truncated version. With some assistance from both the bumptious and the self-doubting Whitman, and with even more assistance from his own archetypal imagination, Crane at once Americanized and transvalued the clown of Laforgue by a poetic method at once ironic and ritualistic. The resulting figure does participate in the long-standing modern view of art as derided and humanity as debased, but he also participates in a much more ancient view. In his very shabbiness and clownishness, as he submits to the transfiguring moon, he represents for a second that moment just prior to an immense inversion of values whereby the humble shall be exalted, the foolish become the source of wisdom, and the world shall renew itself by honoring the ridiculous, the disgraced, the outlaw.

If there is one event above all others that is truly significant in European and American literature in the past few decades, it is something of just that sort. It has been marked by a continuing exploration of the lowest of the low to find and expose elements of the highest of the high, to dig in the human debris for intimations of mythic grandeur or of sanctity.[22] This is what happens so fleetingly in "Chaplinesque" when the little tramp suddenly makes out by moonlight, in the actual and spiritual slums of the modern world, the holy grail in an empty ash-can; it was to happen again on an incomparably larger scale in *The Bridge*. It is a feat of the visionary imagination by a poet for whom *la lune* really was, once more, *Notre Dame*, an object to be imitated, revered, and trusted in. But the grail is "a grail of laughter," and it is by an extension of comedy that Crane's own bedraggled Harlequin becomes again the Fool of Love in the presence of grace. Just so, in medieval romance, it was the most clownish and uncouth of King Arthur's knights, Sir Percival, who was elected to discover the sacred vessel and fulfill the aspiration of the age.

---

[22] Cf. Northrop Frye's seminal discussion of "ironic literature" in *Anatomy of Criticism* (Princeton, N.J., 1958), and the way the "ironic" mode tends to move back cyclically toward myth.

# ART IN A CLOSED FIELD

by

## HUGH KENNER

Fed with a vocabulary of 3,500 words and 128 different patterns of simple-sentence syntax, the computer can turn out hundreds of poems. . . . The words it picks from have to be kept in separate boxes —all nouns together, all verbs, etc. But by drastically cutting down its choice of words—so that the incidence of a subject word reappearing is greatly increased—engineers can make the machine seem to keep to one topic.

*Time*, May 25, 1962

# T

HAT MACHINES INVENTED
to help us with our arithmetic should
indulge in a few hundred harmless doodlings with
language—

All girls sob like slow snows.
Near a couch, that girl won't weep.
Stumble, moan, go, this girl might sail on the desk.
This girl is dumb and soft.

—is nothing to excite surprise. It is normal for terri-
tories the imagination has once pioneered to be occupied at last by hardware, as Lockean psychology
prepared the way for camera and data-file. What

seems not to have been much studied is the way creative writers and creative mathematicians have been exploring comparable processes, of which the engineers' Auto-Beatnik is merely a late and novel byproduct.

I am going to argue (1) that the recent history of imaginative literature—say during the past 100 years —is closely parallel to the history of mathematics during the same period; (2) that a number of poets and novelists in the last century stumbled upon special applications of what I shall call, by mathematical analogy, the closed field; (3) that this principle has since been repeatedly extended to produce wholly new kinds of literary works; and (4) that it is worth knowing about and of general applicability because it helps you make critical discoveries, by which I mean, that it helps you to think more coherently and usefully about the literature of both our own time and times past.

More than twenty-five years ago there was performed at the University of Wisconsin a piece of research, as a result of which it is now possible to say with some confidence what Joyce's *Ulysses* contains.[1] It contains 29,899 different words, of which 16,432 occur only once apiece. At the other end of the scale, the commonest word, which is the definite article, is used no fewer than 14,877 times, and altogether the reader of *Ulysses* passes his eye along slightly more than a quarter of a million separate words, of which just 9 begin with the letter X.

[1] Miles L. Hanley *et al.*, *Word-Index to James Joyce's Ulysses* (Madison, Wis., 1937).

Now you could make the same kind of statement about any book whatever, and it would merely be interesting, perhaps not very interesting. But most students of Joyce's text would probably grant that when Professor Hanley and his team of indexers at Wisconsin took *Ulysses* apart into separate words and studied and classified and counted those words, they were doing something oddly similar to whatever Joyce was doing when he put the book together in the first placc. The closed set of words which we call the book's vocabulary was most deliberately arrived at. It was not simply Joyce's own vocabulary, but one that he compiled. And the rules by which the words are selected and combined are not the usual rules that used to be said to govern the novelist. The traditional novelist is governed by some canon of verisimilitude regarding the words people actually use and by a more or less linear correspondence between the sequence of his statements and the chronology of a set of events. In *Ulysses* the events are very simple and are apt to disappear beneath the surface of the prose; the style, as the book goes on, complicates itself according to laws which have nothing to do with the reporting of the visible and audible. Again and again we find Joyce inserting a word or a combination of words precisely so that he can allow it to carry a motif, as in music, by simply repeating it on a future page. System, in fact, sometimes took precedence over lexicography. Thus when Frank Budgen pointed out, while an early episode was in manuscript, that sails are not brailed up to crosstrees but to yards, Joyce had nevertheless no choice: "The word 'crosstrees' is essential. It comes in later on and I can't change it."[2]

We are talking about *Ulysses* in the way Joyce at that moment was thinking of it: as a set of pieces and some procedures for arranging them. We have the author's sanction for supposing that this is one profitable way to think about *Ulysses* and we shall be coming back to it. Let us first extend the principle a little further. For it seems that one can multiply without effort out of the literature and criticism of this century example after example of the habit of regarding works of art as patterns gotten by selecting elements from a closed set and then arranging them inside a closed field. Put this way, it sounds like a game; and my first example is the book Miss Elizabeth Sewell devoted to the world of Lewis Carroll, whose works are structured with card games and chess games. Her book is suggestively titled *The Field of Nonsense*. Before the exposition has gone very far she is talking of "the tight and perfect little systems of Nonsense verse pure and simple," and before the page is finished she has invoked *la poésie pure* and the name of Mallarmé.[3]

Carroll, she suggests, is "the English manifestation of the French logic and rigor which produced the work of Mallarmé, also labeled nonsense in its time. Carroll is perhaps the equivalent of that attempt to render language a closed and consistent system on its own; but he made his experiment not upon Poetry but upon Nonsense." Now the field of Nonsense, she goes on to show, is not blur and fusion but separation

[2] Frank Budgen, *James Joyce and the Making of Ulysses* (Bloomington, Ind., 1960), p. 56.
[3] London, 1952, p. 21.

and control. Its field is, once more, the closed field, within which elements are combined according to specified laws. "The process," Miss Sewell writes, "is directed always towards analysing and separating the material into a collection of discrete counters, with which the detached intellect can make, observe and enjoy a series of abstract, detailed, artificial patterns of words and images. . . . All tendencies towards synthesis are taboo: in the mind, imagination and dream; in language, the poetic and metaphorical elements; in subject matter, everything to do with beauty, fertility, and all forms of love, sacred and profane."

Miss Sewell hazards that we may be reminded of the New Criticism; certainly she is reminded of the New Poetry, and in a remarkably suggestive essay she applies her entire theory of Nonsense to the author of "The Waste Land,"[4] that poem which so separates its materials that the problem for the novice reader, who generally has trouble analyzing poems, is in this case to get the parts back together again; that poem, furthermore, which comes upon themes of beauty, fertility, and all forms of love, sacred and profane, with so sidelong and detached a self-sufficiency. And her formulation may also remind us of the New Novel, the novel since Flaubert, who made a cult, we know, of the Exact Word.

The closed field contains a finite number of elements to be combined according to fixed rules. In order to get a closed field you have to have its elements, and it was Flaubert who took this particular

[4] Elizabeth Sewell, "Lewis Carroll and T. S. Eliot as Nonsense Poets," in Hugh Kenner, ed., *T. S. Eliot: A Collection of Critical Essays* (Englewood Cliffs, N.J., 1962), pp. 65-72.

step. It was he who defined the element of the novel as not the event but the word, just as it was Mallarmé who said that poems were made of words, not ideas. Consider Flaubert and the single word for a moment. I do not discover his particular mode of interest in the single word in earlier writers. Flaubert is very adept at making us *see* a common word for the first time. He is equally adept with a very large vocabulary of special-purpose words, whose air of uniqueness can attest to an accuracy of observation for which stock parts would not suffice. When he assimilates words into idioms, it is because he wants us to notice the idiom, which is commonly a borrowing or a parody. Now Flaubert's interest in the isolated word is the residue of nearly two centuries of lexicography, which had virtually transformed the vocabulary of each written language into a closed field. The dictionary takes discourse apart into separate words, and arranges them in alphabetical order. It implies that the number of words at our disposal is finite; it also implies that the process by which new words are made has been terminated. Hence the persistent lexicographical concern, from Johnson's day to nearly our own, with fixing the language. That Shakespeare had no dictionary and that he was less occupied with words than with a continuous curve of utterance are corollary phenomena. That Scott and Dickens, surrounded by dictionaries, still manifest little curiosity concerning the single word is no contradiction to what we have been saying, but simply testimony to the domination of their discourse by oral models; they think of a man telling a story. But Flaubert, the connoisseur of the *mot juste*, comes to terms with the fact that whatever printed discourse may be modeled on, it is assembled out of the constituents of the written language; and the written language has been analyzed, by a long process which took its inception with the invention of printing, into Miss Sewell's two desiderata: a closed field, and discrete counters to be arranged according to rules.

Let us remark in passing the essential absurdity which menaces this procedure. Though it obeys with clear-sighted fidelity the inherent laws of written discourse, laws which have struggled out of a long latency into explicit visibility, yet it affronts, satirizes, criticizes, frequently insults, the principles of the spoken language, the principles of the world in which language takes its origin and has its essential and continuing use: the world, we are apt to forget, where the written language has a very minor, and certainly not a dominant, place. Here is the fulcrum of that strain between fiction and what is called "life," even the verbal part of "life," which is explored with increasing freedom by a succession of writers from Flaubert to Beckett. Flaubert is especially fond of bringing the written and spoken languages into each other's presence when his characters are talking, and what he exploits of the written language is its air of being synthesized out of little pieces. Books, it seems, can do nothing to human behavior except contaminate it, and contaminate it with cliché. A cliché is simply an element from the closed field. When Emma Bovary says that there is nothing so admirable as sunsets, but especially by the side of the sea, she is not feeling but manipulating the counters of a synthetic feeling, drawn from reading. And Flaubert, it is well known, in carrying such principles yet further, even made lists of clichés and proposed to arrange them in alphabetical order by key words, defining, so, the closed field of popular discourse, the pieces of which are phrases as the writer's pieces are single words. And it is unnecessary to speak of his closed field of character: three types of adulterer, for example, two types of bourgeois; or his closed field of event, a very small field indeed. Everything throughout his novels is menaced by the débâcle of the absolutely typical; "Bouvard and Pécuchet" does but repeat the same small cyclic motion, study, enthusiasm, practice, disaster, over and over until it has used up all the things that the curriculum affords us to study: a closed field of plot consuming a closed field of material.

It is clear that the various closed fields in which a Flaubert may deploy his fictional energies are supplied from various directions, to be superimposed, several of them at a time, in the achieved novel. The notion of language as a closed field may be attributed to the dictionary and behind it to the printing press, which insists, as does its domesticated version the typewriter keyboard, that we have at our disposal less certainly the possibly infinite reaches of the human spirit than twenty-six letters to permute. The notion of character as a closed field is traceable to the prestige of several sorts of long-range and short-range causality—historical, sociological, psychological. The notion of a closed field of significant events reflects, perhaps, the theories of probability which have been resourcefully explored and increasingly publicized from Pascal's day to ours. We are all of us accustomed, in fact, to the postulates of the closed field, and it is within this set of habits we have formed that the art to which we are most responsive takes its course.

Here we should return to Joyce. We may take *Ulysses* to specify one arrangement, and in the author's judgment the most significant arrangement, of all the ways its quarter-million words might be arranged. Were we to say the same of a novel of Walter Scott's, it would be merely a theoretical statement, but when we say it of *Ulysses*, we feel we are saying something relevant to the book's nature. Joyce wrote in the midst of an economy of print, surrounded by other books on which to draw. He possessed, for example, Thom's Dublin Directory for the year 1904. He possessed dictionaries in which to find the day's words and verify their spelling. He possessed other books in which he could find lists of all kinds: the colors of mass vestments, for instance, and their significance.

Discourse, for Joyce, has become a finite list of words, and Dublin, 1904, in the same way has become the contents of Thom's Directory, in which it was possible for Joyce to verify in a moment the address of every business establishment or the occupancy of every house (he was careful to install the Blooms at an address which, according to Thom's, was vacant). Theoretically, it would have been possible for him to name somewhere in *Ulysses* every person who inhabited Dublin on that day. Dublin, 16 June 1904, is documented in the newspapers of the day; Profes-

sor Richard Kain has shown with what care Joyce
assimilated the names of the horses who were racing
in the Gold Cup, or the details of the American steam-
boat disaster which occupied the Dublin headlines that
evening. Even the nine participants in a quarter-mile
footrace are embalmed forever in his text, name by
name: M. C. Green, H. Thrift, T. M. Patey, C. Scaife,
J. B. Jeffs, G. N. Morphy, F. Stevenson, C. Adderly,
and W. C. Huggard.

And we may note the congruence of such lists with
other finite lists. There are twenty-four hours in a
day, and he accounts for all but the ones spent by his
characters in sleep. The spectrum has seven colors,
and Bloom names them: roy g biv. The *Odyssey* can
be dissociated into specific episodes, which Joyce accounts for. Shakespeare wrote some thirty-six plays;
I do not know whether Joyce includes in the library
scene an allusion to each of them, but it would not
be surprising. The embyro lives nine months in the
womb, or forty weeks; the body of the "Oxen of the
Sun" episode has nine principal parts, in forty para-
graphs, linked furthermore to a sequence of geological
eras obtained from a list in a textbook. To adduce
lists, to enumerate or imply the enumeration of their
elements, and then to permute and combine these elements—this, Joyce seems to imply, is the ultimate
recourse of comic fiction.

Such a diagnosis is confirmed by the procedures of
Joyce's most intelligent disciple, Samuel Beckett.
Beckett's second novel, *Watt*, has for point of departure the great catechism in the seventeenth episode
of *Ulysses*, and repeatedly it defines, with frigid de-

liberation, closed fields the elements of which it dog-
gedly permutes through every change that system can
discover.

Here he stood. Here he sat. Here he knelt. Here he lay.
Here he moved, to and fro, from the door to the window,
from the window to the door; from the window to the
door, from the door to the window; from the fire to the
bed, from the bed to the fire; . . .

and so on, until each possible route between bed, door,
window, and fire has been traced in each direction.
The point is that system must supplement our very
scanty knowledge of Mr. Knott and, nothing system
has to say being open to challenge, a considerable
number of true propositions can be accumulated. It
is understood that the reader's principal concern is to
acquire knowledge of the shadowy Mr. Knott, who
seems a first adumbration of the still more mysterious
Mr. Godot, and it is a surly reader who will complain
of the cognitive riches that system showers upon him.
Later in the book Watt commences some experiments
of his own with the closed field. Given a brief vocabulary of English monosyllables, he first inverts the order of the words in the sentence, and then the order
of the letters in the word, and later that of the sentences in the period; then he performs simultaneously
each possible pair of inversions in this set of three,
and finally he combines all three inversions simultaneously, thus subjecting his little store of monosyllables to every, literally every, possible process of
inversion. With a little effort we find we can get used
to any of these conventions of discourse. None of
them approaches a merely random sprinkling of vo-

cables, though each of them reminds us sharply of the perilous random seas that surround our discourses.

It might at this point be objected that we are in the presence of nothing more significant than Joyce implying a method, and Beckett playing with it. But I think it can be shown that we have come upon something much more pervasive than that. I think, in fact, that the conditions of the closed field have been infiltrating our thought processes for some decades, and that the analogy I have been proposing, an analogy which I have shown to be deliberately wielded by several eminent writers of fiction, has perhaps already become the dominant intellectual analogy of our time. We use it to lend structure and direction to our thoughts, as the Victorians used biology and as the men of the Enlightenment used Newtonian physics. The closed field is a mathematical analogy. Let me put this as flatly as possible: the dominant intellectual analogy of the present age is drawn not from biology, not from psychology (though these are sciences we are knowing about), but from general number theory.

Let no one be frightened by talk about General Number Theory. I have only three things to say about it, none of them esoteric. First, it is from the terminology of general number theory that the word "field" seems to have found its ways into such discussions as ours. My second statement has to do with the way the mathematician uses the word "field." A field, he says, contains a set of elements, and a set of laws for dealing with these elements. He does not specify what the elements are. They may be numbers, and the laws may be the laws that govern addition and multiplication. But numbers are a special case; in the general case the elements are perfectly devoid of character, and we give them labels like *a*, *b*, and *c*, so as to keep track of them. The laws, in the same way, are any laws we like to prescribe, so long as they are consistent with one another. The purpose of this maneuvre is to set mathematics free from our inescapable structure of intuitions about the familiar world, in which space has three dimensions and every calculation can be verified by counting. Once we have a theory of fields we can invent as many mathematical systems as we like, and so long as they are internally consistent their degree of correspondence with the familiar world is irrelevant. It seems illuminating to note that once you shift the postulates of the novel a little, you can have a book like *Ulysses*, but as long as you adhere to the common-sense view that a novel tells a story, *Ulysses* is simply impossible. And my third remark about number theory is this, that its concept of the field is a device for making discoveries. At first it seems to make mathematics wholly irresponsible, and then it permits a whole stream of non-Euclidean and transfinite systems; finally these queer mental worlds do turn out to describe the familiar world after all, but from an angle the existence of which we should never have suspected. The classic example is the geometry invented by Lobachevski which uses four of Euclid's five postulates but reverses the one about parallel lines; it hung around, an intellectual curiosity, until its practical use was discerned by Einstein.

It seems useful to say of the literary arts in the past

hundred years that they have undergone a strikingly similar development. For centuries literature, like arithmetic, was supposed to be, in a direct and naive way, "about" the familiar world. But lately we have been getting what amounts to the shifting of elements and postulates inside a closed field. I have mentioned the example of *Ulysses*, and I might mention several more; for instance, if you drop the assumption that novels are more about people than they are about things, you open up the field where the novels of Robbe-Grillet are composed.

All this may seem too general to be of any use to the literary critic, so I had better give a few illustrations which tend to indicate how, on the contrary, a critic may find field theory highly useful. My first example should be above suspicion, since it concerns a critic who has already employed the theory to a- chieve what is widely agreed to be a most valuable result. I mean the British critic Donald Davie, and the book he wrote a dozen years ago on diction, in which he succeeded in moving the concept of diction for- ward from the handbook commonplace that Diction is the writer's Choice of Words.[5] This is one of the most unhelpful of commonplaces, for since we knew beforehand that the words were supposed to have been chosen, there seems to be no point in introduc- ing a term to emphasize the fact. Mr. Davie made the term useful and illuminating by invoking the analogy of the closed field, and to illustrate how pervasive this analogy has become, I should add that he does not

[5] Donald Davie, *Purity of Diction in English Verse* (New York, 1953).

explicitly identify it and may have been unaware of
its source. What he said was this. Let us compare a
writer like Shakespeare, who we intuitively feel does
not employ a specifiable diction, with a writer like
Pope, who does. Can we not put our intuition in this
form, that certain words exist, indeed a very large
class of words exists, which Pope, however many
poems he wrote, would never employ? And have we
not the further certainty that any conceivable word
might well, for all we know, turn up in Shapespeare's
usage, and at any moment? From these propositions
Mr. Davie moves to his definition of a diction, which
may be paraphrased like this: A diction is a selection
of language from which the words the poet uses in
this poem are in turn selected. This poem may con-
tain, say, 400 words, but we can sense that these 400
words were drawn, not indiscriminately from the
entire resources of the language, but from a special
portion of it; and that special portion we call a diction. It is a subfield; and when the writer leaves us
with no special awareness of his diction, it is because
his practice does not urge us to intuit such a subfield.
Behind Mr. Davie's illuminating pages lies the notion
of the closed field from which elements are selected,
a closed field coextensive with the language itself in
the case of Shakespeare, more restricted in the case
of Pope. This analogy—let me emphasize that it *is* an
analogy, since it is surely not going to be urged that
there exists anywhere a list of the words from which
Pope selected—this analogy illuminates the concept
of diction.

I should add that what Mr. Davie does for the poets

who employ a diction (he was thinking specifically of the poets of the mid-eighteenth century) can be done for all writers, and usefully done, if you make your criteria general enough. It is very helpful, I find, to regard a work of art as proceeding according to certain rules (did not Coleridge say that it contains *within itself* the reason why each detail is so and not otherwise?). The rules may be changed beyond easy recognition by altering one postulate, and this is a common way for the arts to develop, although it is perhaps only now, with the assistance of field theory and game theory, that it is possible to see clearly that this is what has been going on. And the first business of the critic is to recover the rules of the game that is laid before him. When Joyce applied to works of literature the scholastic terms, *integritas, consonantia, claritas*, he made the phase of enlightenment *claritas*, depend on the two preceding phases: *integritas*, the perception that the work is indeed a unity, and *consonantia*, the tracking of its internal laws. I am adding to this analysis only one thing, that the innovator commonly changes a familiar law or two, and in so doing defines a closed field of possible works within which his own work finds its place.

For my last examples I want to open up an International Theme. The writers we have been discussing are all Europeans, and the closed field as we have been exploring it has a European ring. It issues in sombre comedy: sombre because, as Eliot indicated in composing "The Waste Land" out of the fragments of previous poems, European arts have been marked for some generations now by the conviction that the game of civilization consists of a delimited number of moves, which are getting exhausted. You will remember that for Eliot the field of literature is only provisionally closed, since it was to incorporate "The Waste Land" itself as soon as "The Waste Land" was finished; I need not remind you of the argument of "Tradition and the Individual Talent," with its talk of monuments, presumably a finite number of them, occupying an ideal order and rearranging themselves somewhat to accommodate a new member.

American literature, however, has always tended to reject such a set of analogies as we have been exploring. That is one reason, I think, why so much recent American poetry has patterned itself aggressively on speech, not print, and furthermore not the speech of conversation, which is always in danger of falling into a closed set of patterns, as Flaubert saw, but rather the speech of what is sometimes called spontaneity but is actually just naked *utterance*, spontaneous or premeditated. That is because it cannot afford to imply an answer, which implies a counteranswer, which implies a conversation, which implies a game with rules and so (as Miss Sewell has indicated, writing of Nonsense) a closed field. A poem by William Carlos Williams is speech all the time, but either it is not speech we are to think of as spoken *to* anyone, but merely *uttered,* or else it is spoken to his wife or an intimate friend, someone who might answer out of hidden depths of intimacy with the poet, but never according to a social stereotype. On further reflection we can see why the speech situations of Creeley and Zukofsky are so domestic, sometimes embarrassingly so, and why Whitman is so often to be detected bullying the reader into intimacy. Whitman seems intuitively to have grasped how the decorums of conversation would enclose his Nuovo Mundo expansiveness in a closed field he did not want, and Williams, Creeley, and Zukofsky have devoted three careers to refining this principle. We may also note that when Mr. Eliot classified possible utterances into words spoken to oneself, to another or some others, or to God, he was leaving no room whatever for what Whitman and Williams were doing. Mr. Eliot was speaking as an American who has assumed European categories.

There is a whole set of critical puzzles which involve the meaning of the word "tone." I. A. Richards defined tone many years ago as the speaker's attitude to the hearer, whereas "feeling" is the speaker's attitude to his subject. This works well enough with a poem like "To His Coy Mistress," but to make it work all the time you have to supply the concept of an audience implied by the poem, even when the poem does not specify that audience. This extension in turn gets into trouble, since a poet like Williams does have an identifiable tone which remains difficult to define. But here closed-field theory comes to our aid; for as soon as we see that a speaker-audience relation implies just exactly the closed field Williams is anxious to evade, avoid, and that he is consequently trying to do without such a relation, and turn the poem into an autonomous utterance, then we see that what he is doing must be governed by a set of laws proper to the utterance, which are not the same laws as the familiar laws that govern discourse. We see, in short, that to avoid confining his art by the set of laws which in Europe artists have been deriving from the world around them and its image of itself, Dr. Williams has devised a new set; and the job of the Williams critic is to discover and state what these are.

My final example is Eliot's friend, the other great American poet to attempt to build a bridge between his country and Europe; a poet, furthermore, who was always careful never to close off the field in which Dr. Williams and Whitman were operating: I mean, of course, Ezra Pound.

Pound has reserved to himself many freedoms; the freedom to continue with the "Cantos" until he has finished them, without being bound by a specified number or scheme; the freedom to ransack libraries and languages; the freedom to incorporate any, but any, level of diction, of tone, of subject, personal or public. You may trace all that side of him to Whitman if you like, or to his affinity for high Bohemia, or simply to his need for elbow room. But he assumes all the time a closed field all the same, and that closed field is the curriculum. The "Cantos," of course, is a didactic work, the work of a university man who nearly turned into a professor. I want to suggest, in concluding, its highly American quality, which suffices to turn the closed field inside out, and make it an instrument of possibilities, not foreclosures.

What we have in the "Cantos" is, first of all, a highly compressed anthology, beginning with Homer. It reflects Pound's interest in the emperor who perceived that there were too many Noh plays and trimmed the

number down, or the legendary anthologist—it used
to be thought Confucius himself—who reduced the
canon of Chinese folk song to just over three hundred
specimens, or perhaps the committee under Pisistratus
that edited the Homeric compilations into their present form. But there are examples nearer home: Mr.
Adler's hundred Great Books, President Eliot's five-
foot shelf. The latter it is easy to see as comic phenomena, mail-order culture. The comedy is modified
when we reflect that all American learning has been
literally mail-order. The first settlers were in the position of the proverbial man who must decide which
twelve books to take to a desert island, and the most
learned of them had to make choices. If they brought
along an Iliad or a Shakespeare, it was deliberately,
after much weighing of options. Everything else had
to be ordered from Europe. Pound has preserved in
the "Cantos" the remarkable letter in which Jefferson
requested from the old world a gardener who could
play the French Horn.[6] It is picturesque, but a frontier
civilization is always picturesque: Jefferson needed
both gardening and music, and hoped to combine
them. It is worth noting that in such a situation you
cannot simply yearn after music, you must know in
detail what you want next: a French horn, or a cello,
or finally perhaps a Toscanini.

The first American universities were founded with
gifts of books, and every American library since then
has reflected a long series of deliberate acts of choice.
A library like the Bodleian contains hundreds of thousands of books; nobody knows how most of them got

[6] *The Cantos of Ezra Pound*, Canto XXI.

there. If many of those same books are in collection
at Yale or Harvard, it is because they were chosen
and ordered for people who had some immediate use
for them. For the same reason, American education
is focused, as European education is not, on the curriculum. The curriculum is an act of selection. Europe is what we know, Europe plus our own past;
but this knowledge is kept current by deliberate acts
of transmission and selection, by continuous teaching,
by rigorous exclusion and concentration, by a constant search for basic books, for the things we should
know before we go on to learn other things, by a
constant re-examination of the active bases of our
knowledge. The library and the curriculum support
one another; the library grows as the curriculum demands.

From this point of view, the kind of act performed
by the poet of the "Cantos" parallels the act which
for three centuries has constituted the continuing cultural history of the United States: selection, definition, choice, imposed first by frontier circumstances,
later by pedagogical necessity, and finally by national
habit. Even our book reviews imply a curriculum;
they tell us whether to read a book or not. The British
reviewer seems to assume that his audience reads everything, or may read everything, and welcomes chat
about it; or else, what amounts to the same thing, that
they read nothing and want access to the mastications
of someone who does.

What happens in the "Cantos," in short, is the deliberate imposition of the closed field on material virtually infinite. Again we are saying something that is

theoretically true of any book whatever, but in this case is relevantly true, relevantly elucidative of the work's nature. And this closed field, since it implies that what is left out the author has examined and determined not to put in, offers to sharpen our attention rather than mock at our poverty of resource. Flaubert, Joyce, Beckett are the Stoic comedians of our recent literature; what Pound seems to be implying is an adventurous comedy instead, a comedy of discovery. It is not for nothing that he loosely follows Dante, who was also a man pursuing a curriculum, under the tutorship of Virgil. What the mathematicians implied when they invented the term in the first place was that the closed field is the condition of learning, as Confucius waved aside the days and nights he had spent in sleepless meditation, with the remark that he would have done better to be studying something in particular.

We are left with the makings of a paradox, which may be stated in the following way. Beckett in one of his novels has Molloy sit on the beach to meditate a problem of groups and cycles.[7] He has before him the elements of a closed field, sixteen stones, and his problem is to suck on each of them, and suck on each in turn until he has completed the set, and then begin again, without duplication; and he will neither number the stones, nor contrive sixteen pockets to put them in. He has four pockets only, and the problem is as heavy as the sort of problem that confronted Newton when he was required to invent the calculus. The whole point of the image, I think, is this: that in suck-

[7] Samuel Beckett, *Molloy* (New York, 1955), pp. 93-100.

ing sixteen stones, however systematically, there is appeasement of a kind, and satisfaction of a kind, particularly satisfaction of the instinct for order, but there is no nourishment. Yet in reading Beckett's account of this operation there is not only laughter, but also nourishment for the affections and the intellect; and it seems perfectly appropriate that we have been quick, in America, to place Mr. Beckett on our curricula. One way or another, when it is focused by art, the closed field becomes that point of concentration which in proportion as it grows smaller concentrates more intensely the radiant energies of all that we feel and know.

# THE
# DISMEMBERMENT OF ORPHEUS

*Notes on Form and Antiform
in Contemporary Literature*

by

IHAB HASSAN

If confusion is the sign of the times, I see at the root of this confusion a rupture between things and words, between things and the ideas and signs that are their representation.

ANTONIN ARTAUD

MODERN LITERATURE IS THE enormous dream of men haunted by the mortality of their gods. But in dreams, the poet said, begin responsibilities. The enormity of modern literature springs from the soul of men and moves in the very life of their culture; with this knowledge begin all responsibilities. Yet most of us look upon the mangled figures who possess the literary imagination of our time as if they were an alien breed. Even madmen know better than thus to elude their fate. Antonin Artaud was at times mad, and he saw the point with pitiless clarity: "What is most important . . . is not

so much to defend a culture whose existence has
never kept man from going hungry [he was not thinking of our bellies], as to extract, from what is called
culture, ideas whose compelling force is identical with
that of hunger."

My general purpose in this essay is to reflect on a
strain of modern literature which, in its agonistic relation to culture, endeavors to extract from it the force
of hunger, the force of desire. My specific aim will
be to comment on the strategy of that literature in
its labor to derive life from enforced deprivation, a
strategy which leads literature from radical distortions
of form to a parody of self-repudiation, and from the
latter to a verbal equivalent of silence. Moden literature protests against the idea of culture; the ultimate
protest of language is silence; the literature of silence
entertains wordlessness for its future. This is the stark
outline.

The outline is stark and the statements excessive;
our road may not lead to Blake's palace of wisdom.
Yet excess is not the only risk we run. In a particular
sense, the literature of silence is not simply extreme,
it is also subversive. For without language, history
and society cease to exist, and civilization reverts to
aboriginal darkness. According to the Gospel, in the
Beginning was the Word, and human life became
possible when the Word was made Flesh. Is the human race, then, which has come such a long and
terrible way through the passages of prehistory, to
be now turned back by some erratic dream? Quite
the contrary. Modern literature may be extreme and
its dreams outrageous, but it is conceived in the in-

terests of life, which always progresses through contradictions. Two major trends, working now in un-
easy unison and now in exuberant opposition, testify
to this fact. The first trend reveals a growing disaffection with modern civilization, a profound grum-
bling which expresses itself rather superficially in
adolescent violence, hipster anarchy, and Oriental
mysticism. The second trend, intimately related to
the first, is founded on a distrust of language as a
medium of expression and a distrust of form, which
has impelled certain modern writers to cultivate chance
and disorder as legitimate elements of the artistic
process, or to evolve patterns of nonsense that may
be called antiform. The suspicion of language reflects
a more radical mistrust of reason, history, and social
organization. At bottom, the revolt is directed against
those inseparable twins, Authority and Abstraction.
For authority in social life and abstraction in language
are corollaries: they are commandments issued to the
flesh, coercing private experience into objective order. The two trends, we see, are aspects of the same
quenchless feud. What is that feud?

Here I revert to the parable of my title. It is the
death of Orpheus, first among singers, that provides
a focus to the story. There are, of course, many versions of the story, though all are equally gory. Orpheus is killed by the Maenads at the behest of Dionysus or, in Ovid's version, in a fit of uncontrollable
jealousy; for since the death of his wife Eurydice,
Orpheus had preferred the company of young men
to women. One thing is clear: Orpheus, the supreme
maker, was the victim of an inexorable clash between

the Dionysian principle, represented by the frenzied Maenads, and the Apollonian ideal which he, as a poet, venerated. We do not really need a motive or excuse for the murder. The maker of songs offended the primal forces of life; he is overwhelmed by them. Ovid describes the scene thus:

> Mad fury reigned, and even so, all weapons
> Would have been softened by the singer's music,
> But there was other orchestration: flutes
> Shrilling, and trumpets braying loud, and drums,
> Beating of breasts, and howling, so the lyre
> Was overcome, and then at last the stones
> Reddened with blood, the blood of the singer, heard
> No more through all that outcry.[1]

Orpheus pays for his "crime" against Dionysus with dismemberment. But the act of dismemberment is also a crime against Apollo, patron of culture, that demands both retribution and restitution. The Meanads cannot wash their bloody hands in the river Helicon which dives horrified into the ground; in one account, they are turned into twisted trees. This is retribution. And the head of Orpheus continues to sing, and where his limbs are buried by the Muses, the nightingales sing sweeter than anywhere else in the world. This is restitution. Retribution and restitution; meanwhile, the primordial conflict continues unresolved.

I take the myth of Orpheus to be a parable of the artist in our time. The powers of Dionysus, which our civilization has so harshly repressed, threaten to erupt with a vengeance. In the process, energy may overwhelm order; language may turn into a howl, a

[1] *Metamorphoses*, tr. Rolfe Humphries, Indiana University Press (Bloomington, Ind., 1961), p. 259.

cackle, a terrible silence; form may be mangled as ruthlessly as the poor body of Orpheus was. And yet the haunting question remains, now as on that wild day in the hills of Thrace: must not the head of the poet be severed in order that he may continue to sing? Let me put the question even more bluntly: is it not necessary that life overwhelm art periodically to insure the health, the prevalence, of man? I should like to suggest that an affirmative answer to this question is perhaps more needful at this time than a negative one, and I should also like to propose that we are witnessing in modern literature a movement toward disorder, an attack on form intended to recover a kind of human innocence. Here I end my parable and end my preamble. We can move closer to the subject by more specific cultural, historical, and literary analysis.

The voice of common sense cannot be stilled; it leads to an overwhelming question. Why should the disaffection with civilization in our age be so acute as to drive literature to such extreme measures? The implication is always that intellectuals are baroque worriers, addicted to a pessimism which they impose on their age. Possibly so, though one suspects that our asylums and penitentiaries are full of men who did not worry enough. The question, however, still stands, and until a black Syntopicon of our maladies is compiled, we can only answer it obliquely. Let us begin with a few scattered and unlikely names. What drove Henry Miller, perhaps the most important writer in English today, to take as his motto the inscription: "When I hear the word Culture, I reach for my revolver"? What prompts Nicolas Berdyaev to say, in

*The Fate of Man in the Modern World,* "What is taking place in the world to-day is not a crisis of humanism . . . but the crisis of humanity"?[2] And what leads Robert Ardrey, contemplating the fate of man among ancient fossils and murderous bones, to thus conclude his *African Genesis:* "Man is neither unique nor central nor necessarily here to stay . . . The power of conscience, blind, anti-rational, and acting in alliance with the weapons fixation, will be the responsible force if self-annihilation be the human outcome"?[3] Such statements, like grapeshot, penetrate the flesh in many places. The malady of man is antique; it is compounded by the malady of culture; both may be working toward an unholy climax.

Grapeshot scatters widely. Freud, however, probes the mind with a dagger. In *Civilization and Its Discontents,* Freud shows that society rests on instinctual repression. This much we all know. What we do not always realize is that every act of renunciation in our lives prepares the way for further renunciations. Nor does the matter end there. Freud goes on to argue that civilization, in its innermost dynamics, *requires more and more repression.* The psychic toll of this process is compounded in interest. The implications of this process for literature are crucial. In a shocking and important book, *Life Against Death,* Norman O. Brown begins where Freud ends. Arguing that all sublimation entails a certain degree of negation of the life instincts, Brown concludes thus: "The negative moment in sublimation is plain in the inseparable con-

[2] Ann Arbor, 1961, p. 24.
[3] New York, 1961, pp. 330, 352.

nection between symbolism (in language, science, religion, and art) and abstraction. Abstraction, as Whitehead has taught us, is a denial of the living organ of experience, the living body as a whole . . ."[4] The logic then—and I do not know if it is quite as relentless as both Brown and Freud make it out to be—is that repression begets civilization, civilization begets more repression, more repression begets abstraction, and abstraction begets death. We are moving along the road of pure intelligence which, as Ferenczi thought, is a principle of madness. Is any salvation for the race possible? Brown offers this:

The human ego must face the Dionysian reality, and therefore a great work of self-transformation lies ahead of it. For Nietzsche was right in saying that the Apollonian preserves, the Dionysian destroys, self-consciousness. As long as the structure of the ego is Apollonian, Dionysian experience can only be bought at the price of ego-dissolution. Nor can the issue be resolved by a "synthesis" of the Apollonian and the Dionysian ego. Hence the late Nietzsche preaches Dionysus. . . . The work of constructing a Dionysian ego is immense; but there are signs that it is already under way. If we can discern the Dionysian witches' brew in the upheavals of modern history—in the sexology of de Sade and the politics of Hitler—we can also discern in the romantic reaction the entry of Dionysus into consciousness.[5]

For the neo-Freudians, then, the problem is repression, abstraction, and the solution is the construction of a Dionysian ego. In their view, language ultimately becomes "the natural speech of the body," a phrase adopted from Rilke.

[4] Middletown, Conn., 1959, p. 172.
[5] *Ibid.*, pp. 175f.

But the fact that Brown cites Nietzsche is also relevant, for Nietzsche is indeed the crucial figure in the intellectual history of our time. He is the ancestor of both Freudians and Existentialists, and he is the living mediator between the two movements. Nietzsche's analysis of western civilization offers, therefore, an argument parallel to Freud's, and one that is perhaps even more compelling. For Nietzsche, the root of evil in the modern world is not simply repression, which is wholly instinctual, but also nihilism, a view which acknowledges the conscious human drive to meaning. From the depths of the nineteenth century he proclaimed God dead, and he saw that the crisis of modern man was a crisis of values. "Why has the advent of nihilism become necessary?" Nietzsche asks in *The Will to Power*. And he answers: "because nihilism represents the ultimate logical conclusion of our great values and ideals—because we must experience nihilism before we can find out what values these 'values' really had. We require, at some time, new values." For him, as for contemporary Existentialists, the fundamental problem is obviously one of meaning. Unlike most of them, however, Nietzsche was a utopian. His solution rested on the affluence of life in the Superman. In that Nietzschean view, the ideal of language becomes action, becomes gesture, since the creation of meaning is less a verbal than a vital process.

Obviously then, the prophecies of utopians, whether Freudian or Existentialist, minimize the role of sublimation, and therefore of language. The human Dionysus or the Superman of the future is simply not a loquacious creature. The future, however, is a long way off, and the business of men is neither to rush history nor to end it, but simply to participate in it. Literature always calls our attention to the present in which we participate. It is, therefore, the response of literature to our age, an age of unusual negation, that must command our immediate attention.

What is the response of literature to the culture of abstraction and repression? Let me cite three modern authors who are as different in age and background as possible: Thomas Mann, Albert Camus, and Norman Mailer. Their common theme is danger, a danger to human life, an even graver danger to art. In two of his masterpieces, *Death in Venice* and *Doctor Faustus*, Mann portrays an artist-hero who trifles at his peril with total depravity. Like Orpheus, poor Aeschenbach is destroyed by the passions he had long neglected, yet his head sings on with the voice of Mann himself. The voice is one of consummate irony, rising only to cancel itself in that self-parody which Mann, in his later years, believed to be the only hope of art. The knolwedge of Leverkuhn is even more demonic; we are not surprised to discover that *Doctor Faustus* incarnates the theme of art on the verge of its own impossibility. Later still, Mann ventured into the chartless depths of crime. As Erich Heller put it in *The Ironic German:* "Art tragically laments the loss of its own mystery in *Doctor Faustus*, and gaily reports it to the cosmic police in *Felix Krull*." Gaily is the word, a dreadful gaiety. Ultimately the face of disorder is comic, and the writer who wishes to capture its lineaments finds himself in the position of the notorious Cretan who, by affirming that all Cretans were liars, denied the truth in the process of stating it, or maintained the truth in the process of denying it—no one can tell exactly which. This is the silence of self-irony. With Camus, self-irony raises the question of ontological doubt. In *Resistance, Rebellion, and Death* Camus says, "The hatred of art, of which our society provides such fine examples, is so effective today because it is kept alive by artists themselves. The doubt felt by the artists who preceded us concerned their own talent. The doubt felt by artists of today concerns the necessity of their art, hence their very existence." What is the nature of this doubt that ravages the artist and subverts his art? In the same essay Camus states: "To create today is to create dangerously. Any publication is an act, and that act exposes one to the passions of an age that forgives nothing. . . . The question, for all those who cannot live without art and what it significes, is merely to find out how, among the police forces of so many ideologies . . . the strange liberty of creation is possible."[6] The phrase "police forces of so many ideologies" subsumes all the repressive forms which the human intelligence has evolved in our time. The primary aim of these police forces is to exercise their control, in depth, on the instinctual impulses of man, and in breadth, on the existential freedom of his actions. Apollonian Form finally becomes Abstract Authority. We should not be surprised, therefore, to discover that the doubt of the artist to which Camus refers is the doubt concerning his very *being*, his identity not merely as a maker but also as a man. The reaction to this ontologi-

[6] New York, 1961, p. 251.

cal doubt, I have already hinted, is twofold: the man rebels, and the artist *plays* at repudiating his art. The close connection between these two aspects of revolt (what the New Critics, may they rest in peace, call the biographical fallacy) is demonstrated by Norman Mailer. In "The White Negro" Mailer describes the "hipster" as

the man who knows that if our collective condition is to live with the instant death by atomic war, relatively quick death by the State . . . or with a slow death by conformity . . . why then the only life-giving answer is to accept the terms of death, to live with death as immediate danger, to divorce oneself from society, to exist without roots, to set out on that uncharted journey into the rebellious imperatives of the self. In short, whether the life is criminal or not, the decision is to encourage the psychopath in oneself, to explore that domain of experience where security is boredom and therefore sickness, and one exists in the present. . . .[7]

Creating dangerously as an artist, the writer must also live dangerously as a man. For art, the risk is total self-repudiation; for man, it is self-annihilation.

Literature in our time confronts the abstract and chilling gaze of Apollo, a deity closer to the Newton of Blake than the gods of the Greeks, and closer still to the image of Dostoevski's Grand Inquisitor. Literature confronts Authority and withers. Should it recoil too far into the Dionysian sources of energy, should it avoid all abstraction and escape all sublimation, it will have expunged the motive for its being. For the Dionysian personality does not choose to live vicariously, nor is it the kind of personality to escape

[7] *Advertisements for Myself* (New York, 1959), p. 339.

abuse. We have lived to see the demented hope of
Marinetti's Futurism consummated by Hitler. "Come
then, seize the pickaxes and hammers! Sap the foun-
dations of the venerable cities. We stand upon the extreme promontories of the centuries . . ." Marinetti
cried, and one visualizes the sullen face of Mars without promise of regeneration. Dionysus does not
prophesy war. What he may prophesy is the complete
wedding of Art and Life, by magic if by nothing else.
Perhaps this is what Pursewarden, the writer in Dur-
rell's *Alexandria Quartet*, meant when he said, "The
object of writing is to grow a personality which in
the end enables man to transcend art." But the end is
not near. We are all still very much in need of art.
The best we can do, as Mailer declared, is to accept
the terms of uncertainty, even of death, which are a
part of our condition. This has been the strategy of
literature in our time. It is a temporary strategy; it
may even be temporizing. Literature recoils from the
withering authority of the new Apollo, but it does
not surrender itself wholly to the frenzy of Dionysus.
It only *feigns* to do so. It employs self-irony and self-
parody, as in the novels of Mann and Camus; it develops, as in the works of Beckett or Genet, forms
that are antiforms; it cultivates a new literalism, as in
the novels of Nathalie Sarraute or Robbe-Grillet; it
evolves the poetic surrealism of John Hawkes and
James Purdy or the collage improvisations of William
Burroughs; and it sometimes entertains a chatty silence
as the later work of Salinger does. Literature, in short,
pretends to a wordy wordlessness and participates in
the Dionysian denial of language not with its own

flesh, but with the irony of its divided intelligence.

So much for the heady response of literature to modern culture. Language aspires to silence and form moves towards antiform. Still, we may find some reassurance in the recognition that the modern phenomenon of antiform has a long and honorable history, and that it is not, therefore, a monstrous child of the moment. Its antecedent may be called the "open form," which is aptly defined by Robert Martin Adams in *Strains of Discord*, as a structure of meanings that "include a major unresolved conflict with the intent of displaying its unresolvedness." An earnest evolutionist may go so far as to claim that just as literature seems to have developed from the mythical to the ironic modes, so do literary forms seem to develop from closed to open forms, and from open forms to antiforms. The distinction between closed and open forms is immediately apparent when we contrast two plays, Sophocles' *Oedipus the King* and Euripides' *Bacchae*. Adams is right in perceiving that while *Oedipus* manages to resolve its conflicts and to induce a state of partial repose in the audience, *The Bacchae* leaves its audience in a state of unreleased anguish. As a closed form, *Oedipus* expresses a conservative and religious view of the world, and a collective sense of experience; as an open form, *The Bacchae* conveys a radical and skeptical view of the world and an individual sense of experience. By extrapolating boldly on this curve, we can say that as an antiform, Beckett's *Waiting for Godot* implies an ironic and nihilistic view of the world and a dream-like sense of experience that is entirely private.

But we need not adhere to a strict theory of literary evolution in order to realize that between *The Bacchae* and *Waiting for Godot* a great number of works in Western literature have revealed a growing sense of disruption, an increasing capacity for distortion. Consider, in drama alone, the sequence suggested by the following plays: Shakespeare's *Hamlet*, Goethe's *Faust*, Büchner's *Woyzeck*, Kleist's *Prinz Von Homburg*, Maeterlinck's *Blue Bird*, Ibsen's *Ghosts*, Strindberg's *A Dream Play*, Jarry's *Ubu Roi*, Pirandello's *Six Characters in Search of An Author*, Brecht's *Man's Man*, Genet's *The Blacks*, and Ionesco's *The Killer*. Dramatic form seems to move from unresolved tensions to symbolic elusiveness, from the latter to surrealistic or expressionistic contortion, and finally comes to rest in absurdity. I limit myself to drama simply to maintain the purity of the illustration. But the movement of form toward antiform, despite large and irrefutable exceptions throughout history, can generally be observed in Western art.

It is probably fair to say that the three major phases of that development were marked by the emergence of Mannerism, Romanticism, and Modernism. Mannerism was the formal dissolution of the Renaissance style. It was, as Wylie Sypher suggests in *Four Stages of Renaissance Style*, a sign of strain and irresolution. In Mannerist art, "the psychological effect diverges from the structural logic." Here is Sypher's definition of what we mean by an open form:

Behind the technical ingenuities of mannerist style there usually is a personal unrest, a complex psychology that agitates the form and the phrase. When we examine the strains within the mannerist structure in painting, architecture, and poetry, we inevitably become aware of the scourge—or the quicksand—within the mannerist temperament. Mannerism is experiment with the techniques of disproportion and disturbed balance; with zigzag, spiral shuttling motion; with space like a vortex or alley; with oblique or mobile points of view and strange—even abnormal—perspectives that yield approximations rather than certainties.[8]

Is not this precisely the feeling we have about Shakespeare's later plays, Jacobean drama, and Metaphysical poetry, as well as the paintings of Titian, Tintoretto, and El Greco?

The Romantics, of course, went further toward unsettling literary forms, haunted as they were by that vague *Stimmung*, the craving for the infinite. *Faust* stands at the very threshold of the period, an amalgam of pagan and Christian influences which it transmuted, both in structure and theme, into a plea for life's outrageous contradictions; only the dazzling genius of Goethe could keep such a drama in artistic control. The dark company of Romantic heroes—Faust, Endymion, Alastor, Don Juan, Julien Sorel, Manfred, Axel—were forever threatening to break out from the mold which contained them, in proud insurrection against their makers. The Self had erupted in literature, and so had the dream and the unconscious. Novalis and Nerval, Hoffmann and Poe, Kleist and Büchner, Coleridge and Keats carried language into the midnight terrain of the soul, or else they cultivated that notorious romantic irony which served to incorporate in every statement its own negative. At other

[8] Garden City, N.Y., 1955, p. 116.

times Romanticism denied itself the possibilities of harmony or resolution by the perversity of its own spirit. It explored sadism, demonism, cabalism, necrophily, vampirism, and lycanthropy, reaching for a definition of man where no human definition could exist. It is no wonder that Goethe thought Romanticism to be a form of disease, and Hugo identified it with the grotesque. I am aware, of course, that I am emphasizing the nocturnal impulse of the movement, but that was precisely the impulse from which a large part of modern literature derived its energy. It was also the impulse, the agony if you wish, which helped to destroy the classic forms of literature. Mario Praz, in *The Romantic Agony*, says, "The essence of Romanticism comes to consist in that which cannot be described. . . . The Romantic exalts the artist who does not give a material form to his dreams—the poet ecstatic in front of a forever blank page, the musician who listens to the prodigious concerts of his soul without attempting to translate them into notes. It is romantic to consider concrete expression as a decadence, a contamination."[9] Here, then, is the beginning of silence, a literature without words, or to be more precise, a literature which disdains all but the most primitive and magical use of language. The French Symbolists, who are, of course, the direct ancestors of the modern movement, exemplify this trend clearly. Mallarmé's sonnets devised the syntax of self-abolition; Rimbaud's *Illuminations* scrambled the denotation of language in an effort to derange the senses; and Lautréamont's *Maldoror* opened the way for sur-

[9] New York, 1956, p. 14f.

realism. It may well be, as Brown claims, that in Romanticism Dionysus re-entered the consciousness of literature. It is more certain that in Romanticism the dual retreat from language became evident: first, in the ironic and self-effacing manner of Mallarmé, and second, in the indiscriminate and surrealistic manner of Rimbaud. In one, language aspires to Nothing; in the other it aspires to All. Both are manners of silence, formal disruptions of the relation between language and reality. It is these two modes, compounded in strange ratios, that account for the development of antiform in modern literature from Kafka to Beckett.

With Modernism, organized chaos reigns; or as Yeats put it,

> the center cannot hold;
> Mere anarchy is loosed upon the world,
> The blood-dimmed tide is loosed....[10]

It is impossible to convey in a few pages the extent of disintegration and re-integration in the major works of our century. In German literature, the frightening indeterminacy of Kafka's works, and in English literature, the over-determinacy of Joyce's later novels, seem to carry the scourge in the language of Mallarmé and Rimbaud into the twentieth century. I do not wish to claim that Mallarmé influenced Kafka, or Rimbaud influenced Joyce, though they may well have done so in the mysterious ways of the creative process. I wish to suggest that the forms of Kafka, like those of Mallarmé, move toward a kind of semantic absence, a total ambiguity; and that the forms of Joyce, like those of Rimbaud, reach for a semantic

[10] *The Collected Poems* (New York, 1957), p. 184.

fullness, a kind of total statement. There is an effort in the first to dissolve reality, and in the second to reconstruct the whole of it. (In this respect, Beckett is far closer to Kafka than he is to his former employer, Joyce). Meanwhile, French literature was steering crazily between these two modes of antiform, veering now toward the one and now toward the other as it rushed through Dadaism, Surrealism, Existentialism, and, most recently, the New Literalism, or Roman Concret, of Butor, Sarraute, Mauriac, and Robbe-Grillet. It is, of course, hopeless to discriminate adequately between all these movements in an article of this scope; our survey must remain a blitz through the literary history of four centuries.

The foregoing survey, however, will not have been totally vain if we recognize that the impulse first to distort, then to inhibit language is a matter of long standing. It defines a strain—a single strain, to be sure, but a significant one—in Western literature. This strain is presently confirmed by a renewed urge to withdraw from the word. Ironically, this urge has been sanctioned not by poetry but science, not by Dionysus but Apollo, not in the interests of the flesh but in the interests of abstraction. In an important article entitled "The Retreat from the Word," George Steiner clarifies the point. He writes:

Until the seventeenth century, the sphere of language encompassed nearly the whole of experience and reality; today, it comprises a narrower domain. It no longer articulates, or is relevant to, all major modes of action, thought, and sensibility. Large areas of meaning and praxis now belong to such non-verbal languages as mathematics, symbolic logic, and formulas of chemical or electronic relation. Other areas belong to the sub-languages or anti-languages of non-objective art and musique concrete. The world of words has shrunk.[11]

This, of course, is largely true. The modern ideologies of men as diverse as Marx, Freud, and Wittgenstein have all served to diminish the powers of language to encompass reality. But Mr. Steiner, I fear, is an Apollonian himself, albeit one of the classical, anthropomorphic sort rather than the modern dehumanized variety. He deplores the state of language in literate society, and thus concludes: "that civilization on which Apollo looks no more shall not long endure."[12] It is my feeling, in this strident era of over-communication, that we are more likely to perish by the word than by the sword, and least of all to perish by a loving silence. But I do not wish to press the point very hard; contemporary literature, far from abdicating its role as a shaper of human consciousness, has accepted the challenge of the enemy. It has, that is, embraced the retreat from the word in order to renew the life of the culture that nourishes it. This development is so recent that it does not yet carry the authority of a major writer. Perhaps its clearest reflection is in that remarkable international movement called the Theatre of the Absurd which includes under one jaunty rubric the works of Beckett, Artaud, Genet, Adamov, Ionesco, Arrabal, Pinter, Gelber, and Albee. No matter what we may think of it as an art form— and I think a good deal of it—we must recognize that

[11] "The Retreat from the Word," *Kenyon Review*, XXIII (Spring, 1961), 203.
[12] *Ibid.*, p. 216.

the movement expresses indirectly nothing less than the desire to redeem Western values. Though the movement may not resurrect Dionysus on the stage before our astonished eyes, Martin Esslin is right when he says, "it is in this striving to communicate a basic and as yet undissolved totality of perception, an intuition of being, that we can find a key to the devaluation and disintegration of language in the Theatre of the Absurd."[13]

Let me end with literary examples somewhat more detailed than any we have viewed so far, and also more close to our situation in America. In reviewing the current literary scene, it becomes quickly obvious that the attack on form and the retreat from language take on a peculiar hue in America. The hue is essentially comic, and it colors the genres of drama, poetry, and fiction. I shall focus mainly on the last.

The new comic spirit in American literature attends a special awareness of reality, a new sense of error and incongruity. It unites horror and slapstick, realism and surrealism, in the most antic manner. Writers nowadays seem anxious to respond to the incoherence of life, to its openness and absurdity. They are relearning the old art of improvisation; they are cultivating the picaresque and the fantastic modes. Knowing how outrageous facts can be, they do not pretend to subdue the intractable stuff of reality with a Jamesian flourish or a mythical symbol. Random operations and radical distortions are accepted in literature not simply as a source of humor, but also as a critique of social goals and traditions. Chance, which defies the

---

[13] *The Theatre of the Absurd* (Garden City, N.Y., 1961), p. 296.

rigid predictability of contemporary life, restores a measure of individual freedom; and distortion defies the habitual response to the world we live in. This is sometimes carried so far as to reveal an anarchic impulse masked in tomfoolery. The clownish element can be sensed in the theatre of Albee and Gelber, the poetry of Corso and Ferlinghetti, the fiction of Kerouac and Burroughs. But it is by no means confined to efforts of the Beats or their associates; it is equally present in such works as Thomas Berger's *Rinehart in Love*, Joseph Heller's *Catch-22*, J. P. Donleavy's *The Ginger Man*, John Hawkes' *The Cannibal*, Saul Bellow's *Henderson the Rain King*, or James Purdy's *Malcolm*. The new comedy, which combines boisterousness and bitterness, is really an attempt to restore sanity through madness or buffoonery. Above all, the new comedy seeks to preserve the health of the community through a qualified tolerance of disorder. Might not the dismemberment of Orpheus prove, after all, to be a comic event?

The connection between the new comedy and new antiforms can be illustrated by three recent works of fiction: Hawkes' *The Cannibal*, Salinger's "Seymour: An Introduction," and Burroughs' *The Naked Lunch*. I have chosen these works because they all possess a certain originality that is not very widely or wisely recognized and because, different as they are, each represents a particular manner of tampering with form. Furthermore, I consider them all to be comic and surrealistic works: comic, in my sense of the word, because they acknowledge the open, indeterminate, or absurd element in human experience, and surrealistic because they tilt and distort the surface of reality in order to express it.

John Hawkes is a striking, and until quite recently, a much neglected writer. He is the author of seven novels and novelettes, of which the best may still be *The Cannibal*, one of the deepest books to come out of World War Two. Like Djuna Barnes or Flannery O'Connor, Hawkes is a specialist in the gothic and grotesque, and his humor is the grim humor of nightmares. He understands the leering comedy of evil and has written, "there is no pathetic fun or mournful frolic like our desire. The consummation of the sparrow's wings." He has also said, "If the true purpose of the novel is to assume a significant shape and to objectify the terrifying similarity between the unconscious desires of the solitary man and the disruptive needs of the visible world, then the satiric writer, running maliciously at the head of the mob and creating the shape of his meaningful psychic paradox as he goes, will serve best the novel's purpose."[14]

In *The Cannibal*, Hawkes' style moves into the twilight region between the rational and absurd. The images are chilly and monstrous. The characters are always out of focus, floating vaguely through a psychic continuum which is neither time nor space. The action is frighteningly simple. A German called Zizendorf is intent on killing the one American soldier, Leevey, who patrols on a motorcycle a third of the entire defeated nation. Both men are equally singleminded and inhuman. There is a town "shriveled in structure and as decomposed as an oxen's tongue black

[14] "Notes on the Wild Goose Chase," *Mass. Review* (Summer, 1962), pp. 786f.

with ants," and there is an insane asylum on a hill. The inmates go berserk, and one of them stalks a child through the novel, just as Zizendorf stalks his prey below. At the end, the lunatic literally devours the child, and Zizendorf kills the soldier. All men are cannibals, whether in love or in hate. A cold frenzy permeates the novel which telescopes the events of 1914 and 1945, dispelling the solidity of the known world with diabolic irrelevance and implacable poetry. And yet the book remains a tangled parable, hard, ruthless, and comic, of the modern world. Its form crystallizes all those distortions prefigured in the flux of man's earliest and blackest recollections. And its language reverts to the syntax of dream or delirium, a crafty mirror of decomposed consciousness.

The act of decomposition is far more whimsical in the work of Salinger. "Raise High the Roof Beam, Carpenters," "Zooey," and "Seymour: An Introduction," present a curious difficulty to the unwary critic. Many feel that the embarrassing mannerisms of these stories—their garrulousness, convolutions, private jokes, and sly asides—betray the fumbling efforts of Salinger to render an experience he has not yet managed to master. I am not of that opinion; I consider the style of these novelettes to be an approximation of comic surrealism, motivated by a sacramental notion of silence. Let me explain. In his earlier work, the dramatic gestures of Salinger's fiction were defined by the poles of love and of squalor. When the gestures aspired to love or pure religious expression, language reached into silence. When the gestures revealed their purely squalid or satiric content, language moved toward sentimentality. In recent years, Salinger has been far more concerned with love than with squalor, and both the language and the antiforms of his stories have been conditioned by an ideal of holiness. The verbal correlative to holiness in Zen is often silence. Salinger, however, is an author, not a Zen master. His task in describing Seymour, a "ringding enlightened man," is to convey in words a life that finds its true consummation in a poetry of silence.

The distrust of language is evident in all these later works. In "Raise High the Roof Beam, Carpenters," Buddy Glass, the narrator, is comforted only by the tiny deaf-mute relative of the bride. Buddy says with disgust, "It was a day, God knows, not only of rampant signs and symbols but of wildly extensive communication via the written word." The profanation of language and spirit are ubiquitous—and identical. The climax of the story comes when Buddy confesses to the deaf-mute, that is, to unhearing ears, the truth about Seymour which he had withheld from all the others. Seymour's own attitude toward language is equally clear in the story: he believes that the Gettysburg Address should have been one man silently shaking his fist at the audience on the occasion of fifty thousand deaths, and he also writes, "the human voice conspires to desecrate every thing on earth." In "Zooey," the same revulsion of language is manifest. Buddy says, "The old horror of being a professional writer, and the usual stench of words that goes with it, is beginning to drive me out of my seat." A crucial insight he receives while talking to a little girl in a supermarket escapes words entirely, and he can only "go through the motions" of writing about it to his brother Zooey. The strange paradox of the stories is that their prolixity seems to undermine, rather than to confirm, the authority of words.

This is perhaps most obvious in "Seymour: An Introduction." In the two earlier stories, language was brilliantly shattered and diffracted: letters, diaries, footnotes, messages scrawled on bathroom mirrors and quotations inscribed on beaverboard, telephone conversations, and endless dialogue dispersed the power of the word, tilting and jumbling the modes of speech. The same practise is exaggerated in "Seymour." Buddy, who is again the narrator, calls himself "a thesaurus of undetached prefatory remarks." The epigraphs to the novelette testify to the inability of language to cope with love. In the quotation from Kafka, love prevents language from exercising its verbal powers, and in the quotation from Kierkegaard, language simply revolts against the author. But the implication is that a true artist will accept the subversion of language in the name of a richer art. Cultivating, as it were, his radical insufficiency, the writer, like Seymour playing marbles, must try not to aim, must try not to try. This is perhaps just what Salinger, in this loose and baggy monster of a narrative, seeks to dramatize. Unpretentious bouquets of "early-blooming parentheses" are offered to the reader; witty exhortations and knowing allusions to Salinger himself, who masquerades as Buddy, follow. "Oh, you out there—" Buddy cries to the reader, "with your enviable golden silence." The novelette has no conventional structure or climax; the portrait of Seymour turns out to be a whimsical catalogue of hair, eyes, ears, and nose. Vignettes follow vignettes almost haphazardly. Language becomes indiscriminate, random, fluent beyond words. And when illumination finally comes to Buddy—one of only five such experiences in his life time—it comes in a purely accidental fashion. Actually, illumination comes to Buddy *because* he had opened himself to accident. Buddy is happy; he has understood himself as a writer because he has understood, with the help of Seymour, the value of suspending purpose. Could it be that the mannered volubility of the novelette is intended to dramatize for us the very same insight: that the happiness of art may lie in the freedom of language to seek some purposeless and indeterminate antiform?

Indeterminacy is carried further in *The Naked Lunch*. This shocking work is sometimes considered the underground masterpiece of the Beat generation. (In a recent Edinburgh Festival, writers as different as Norman Mailer and Mary McCarthy praised it highly.) It is, of course, impossible to describe Burroughs' book and very hard to judge it. The mind reels under the impact of its outrageous vision, its demented language. The ghastly experiences of drug addiction, sexual perversion, and political crime lie at its center, and they seem almost beyond the scope of the human imagination, a satirical nightmare which, like the more shattering works of Swift or Hieronymus Bosch, must be dreamt to be believed. In the terrifying metaphor of junk, "the mold of monopoly and possession" Burroughs seems to have found an expression for solipsism as well as social annihilation. The fiend of narcotics devours everything in the book, devours even the diabolic sexuality that enrages the censors. The "novel" is finally a testament to the insanity of society, the willfulness of the human spirit, and the futility of language, a testament of blood and black laughter. "The title means exactly what the words say," Burroughs writes, "Naked Lunch—a frozen moment when everyone sees what is on the end of every fork."

But the effect of gallows surrealism depends as much on the subject as on the style of the work. The style is unstrung, berserk, splintered. At times it seems a product of what Burroughs calls the "Cut Up Method," which goes back to the surrealist antics of Tristan Tzara. Burroughs describes the method thus:

Method is simple: Take a page or more or less of your own writing or from any writer living and or dead. Any written or spoken words. Cut into sections with scissors or switch blade as preferred and rearrange the sections. Looking away. Now write out the result. . . .

Applications of cut up method are literally unlimited cut out from time limits. Old word lines keep you in old word slots. Cut your way out. Cut paper cut film cut tape. Scissors or switch blade as preferred. Take it to cut city.[15]

There is the method, and there the rationale: "cut your way out!" Neumann's theory of games or the random spirit of Zen are equally valid in freeing man from predetermined forms, from language itself as we have understood it for several millenia of history.

[15] *Casebook on the Beat,* ed. Thomas Parkinson (New York, 1961), pp. 105f.

Hawkes twists and distorts, reaching for the decomposed consciousness of man; Salinger plays with artistic purpose and begins to rely on the silence of diffuseness and improvisation; Burroughs actually employs a random method of composition. The purpose of indeterminacy is the same: cutting the way out. Out of what? Out of history, authority, form, abstraction. Into what? This is a matter each man, with luck, may determine alone.

The story of man, we must aver on faith, is without an ending. The story of literature is equally endless. We cannot gloat over the dangerous act of Orpheus' dismemberment. More than ever we have much to preserve in the human heritage and much to fear from the madness incarnated in history. Men of virtue can not opt for disorder, or choose the terrible darkness of consciousness over the light of courage or devotion. Without language, without form, there can be no human cognition, and without cognition of the self as of the world, there can be no light. We should not revel, therefore, as the mindless Maenads did, in the destruction of Orpheus. In his death, we all die a little. And yet is this not also the Christian, indeed the primordial, paradox of experience: that in symbolic deaths there is renewed life, and in provisional destruction there is the promise of creation?

As a student of literature, I have described a trend toward formlessness and toward wordlessness. But in my view, a critic cannot hold back his moral commitment, he must also stand forth to testify. I therefore add to my description something more than a statement and less than a prescription. I add a plea: that we extend a little of our sympathy to the ordeal of modern literature, that ordeal of dismemberment which is our very own. We live in an age of organized chaos, and we have more to fear from organization than from chaos. The desire to thaw the frozen patterns of our life, to open the forms of our literature or our society, is not merely an artistic aspiration, it is a moral necessity. There is so much that we have allowed habits and fears to exclude from our love; the human reach is shrunken. Yet life still beckons with bright surprise. We can but admire the artist— he is the composer, John Cage—who says, "Our intention is to affirm this life, not to bring order out of chaos nor to suggest improvements in creation, but simply to wake up to the very life we're living, which is so excellent once one gets one's mind and one's desires out of its way and lets it act of its own accord." This is the statement of a man who rejects the tyrannies of art without refusing its exuberance. The artist in Cage is commensurate with the man. Nor will any lesser measure do for audiences who expect to benefit from the bounties of art. No great art can survive without great audiences, and no audiences will survive at all without more quickness, more openness. The story is really a very old one. To hear again, to see again, to feel again, and perhaps sometimes to love what is seen or heard or felt—is this not the whisper of silence in modern literature? Is this not why the head of Orpheus sings on, and his sacrifice is finally justified?

# CONTRIBUTORS

## IHAB HASSAN

Now Professor of English at Wesleyan University in Connecticut, Ihab Hassan was educated at the universities of Cairo and Pennsylvania and holds graduate degrees in both Electrical Engineering and English. He is the author of many articles on contemporary literature and two books: *Radical Innocence, Studies in the Contemporary American Novel,* and *Crises du Héros Americain Contemporain.* On his second Guggenheim Fellowship at present (1963-1964), he is at work on a study of form and antiform in contemporary literature.

## HARRY LEVIN

His first book, *The Broken Column,* was published before he received his A.B. degree from Harvard. Since that time he has published studies of Joyce, Stendhal, Balzac, and Marlowe, and he has also edited works by Jonson, Rochester, Flaubert, Joyce, and Shakespeare. At Harvard he has served as chairman of the Department of Comparative Literature and of the Division of Modern Languages. He has been a visiting professor at the Universities of Paris and Tokyo. Mr. Levin is a Senior Fellow in the Society of Fellows at Harvard and a Chevalier of the Legion of Honor.

# R. W. B. LEWIS

Now Professor of English and American Studies at Yale, he holds degrees from Harvard and the University of Chicago. Mr. Lewis has taught at Bennington, Salzburg, Smith, and Rutgers, and has held fellowships from Princeton, the *Kenyon Review*, the National Institute of Arts and Letters, and the American Council of Learned Societies. His interests range from classical literature to creative writing, and include English, American, and contemporary European literature. He has published widely in periodicals on many subjects. His two books— *The American Adam* and *The Picaresque Saint*—are well known to students of American and contemporary literature.

# HUGH KENNER

A Canadian by birth and a graduate of the University of Toronto and Yale, Mr. Kenner is now Professor of English at the University of California at Santa Barbara. He has written many essays (some of which were collected under the title *Gnomon*) and books on such writers as Pound, Joyce, Wyndham Lewis, Eliot, and Beckett. His latest book, *The Stoic Comedians*, relates the work of Flaubert, Joyce, and Beckett, and develops some of the ideas presented in this essay. He is a contributing editor of the *National Review* and *Poetry*. At present (1963-1964), while in residence as a visiting professor at the University of Virginia, he is working on a study of the Anglo-American literature of 1910-1960, a work to be called *The Pound Era*.

# JOHN FREDERICK NIMS

Poet, translator, teacher, and editor, his career has afforded him many opportunities to combine his various vocations. A teacher at the University of Notre Dame since 1939, Mr. Nims has also been a Fulbright Lecturer in American Literature in Italy from 1952 to 1954 and Visiting Professor of American Studies at the University of Madrid from 1958 to 1960. He has contributed editorial and critical services to *Poetry* magazine in Chicago, translated the works of St. John of the Cross, assisted at Breadloaf writers' conferences, and published several volumes of verse. His most recent book is *Knowledge of the Evening*, published by Rutgers University Press in 1960.

# INDEX

# PETERS RUSHTON
# SEMINAR LECTURES

1. Donald S. Stauffer, "The Poetry of William Butler Yeats," 1946
2. Edwin Berry Burgum, "The Work of James Joyce," 1947
3. Willard Thorp, "The Poetry of T. S. Eliot," 1947
4. Theodore Spencer, "The Poetry of W. H. Auden," 1947
5. Cleanth Brooks, "Poetry in the Age of Anxiety," 1947
6. W. H. Auden, "Poetry and Freedom," 1948
7. René Wellek, "Literature and Ideas," 1948
8. Arthur Mizener, "The Work of F. Scott Fitzgerald," 1948
9. Basil Willey, "The Value of Literary Study to Society and the Individual," 1948
10. A. T. Mollegen, "Some Theological Aspects of Contemporary Poetry," 1949
11. Stephen Spender, "Modern Poetry in the Modern World," 1949
12. Malcolm Cowley, "William Faulkner's Legend of the South," 1949
13. Lionel Trilling, "Art and Neurosis," 1949
14. R. P. Blackmur, "The Lion and the Honeycomb," 1950
15. Caroline Gordon, "The Use of Metaphor in Prose Fiction," 1950
16. Robert Penn Warren, "William Faulkner and his South," 1951

Note: Lecture 33, with the exception of those in this volume, is the only one which is available from the University Press of Virginia.